BEATING THE SYSTEM

BEATING THE SYSTEM

OWEN BOWCOTT
AND
SALLY HAMILTON

BLOOMSBURY

First published in Great Britain 1990
Bloomsbury Publishing Ltd, 2 Soho Square, London WIV 5DE
© Owen Bowcott and Sally Hamilton 1990

A CIP catalogue record for this book is
available from the British Library

ISBN 0 7475 0513 6

10 9 8 7 6 5 4 3 2 1

Typeset by Hewer Text Composition Services, Edinburgh
Printed in Great Britain by Richard Clay Ltd, Bungay, Suffolk

Edward Singh was a college dropout who threatened the security
of some of the most secret and powerful computer systems in the
western world. His obsession led him to pose as a student at the
University of Surrey, where he hijacked their computers to penetrate
banks, universities, multinational companies and atomic weapons
manufacturers. He violated the security of the US Government's
nuclear defence agency where he attempted to play a world war
simulation programme.
Pursued by the US Secret Service and Scotland Yard's Serious Crimes
Squad, he narrowly avoided prosecution under the Official Secrets
Act. His co-hackers were tracked down and accused variously of
spying and extortion.
If current legislation is successful, hacking will soon be illegal in
Britain. *Beating the System* examines the consequences of commercial
and government information being loaded onto interconnected
computer systems, the problems of law enforcement agencies
operating against criminals working from abroad, and the vogue
for viruses. Whatever their potential for harm, hackers highlight
dangerous weaknesses in computer security – problems which anyone
keeping confidential information needs to address.
Beating the System is a hard-hitting analysis of the personalities,
technologies and political issues involved in hacking. It is a work
which no one concerned with the subject can afford to ignore.

PUBLISHERS NOTE
Hacking is likely to be illegal by the summer of 1990.

A NOTE ON THE AUTHORS
Owen Bowcott is a reporter on *The Guardian*. He lives in West
London and previously worked for the *Daily Telegraph* and
Panorama, the BBC current affairs programme.

Sally Hamilton is a reporter on *Business* magazine. She lives in South
London and was formerly on *Computer News* before becoming
features editor of *Computing Magazine*.

ACKNOWLEDGMENTS

The authors would like to thank all those interviewed for their help and time; in particular, Peter Sommer, Jack Schofield, Hans Gliss and Angus McCrone, who contributed valuable advice on computers and computer security, and Alistair Kelman, who provided information on the legal history of hacking. Graham Seaby and Malcolm Padina were happy to explain the repercussions of Edward Singh's activities. We are grateful to Hans Hübner for discussing connections between West German hackers and the Russian trade mission in East Berlin. 'Shatter' and Kevin Hull kindly put us in contact with developments on the Continent. Icon Software of Shepherd's Bush, London, generously helped rescue data savaged by a recalcitrant computer.

CONTENTS

Prologue

HACKERS IN HANDCUFFS

Philadelphia, Pennsylvania: 11 February 1988.

The invitation to a working breakfast in the private suite of the Four Seasons Hotel in downtown Philadelphia was more intimidating than flattering to the twenty-two-year-old computer science student. A room that size must have cost two or three thousand dollars to hire, Scott Klein thought as he was ushered in. Coffee, fruit, cereals, toast and eggs were spread out on a side table. The computer company's personnel officer invited Klein to help himself. Although on his way to college, Klein was too nervous to eat anything. At that moment he was only concerned with signing a contract. This was their third meeting.

The previous month Klein, a devoted computer hacker and a student at Philadelphia's Temple University, had approached the computer company offering his services as a security consultant. Hacking into their networks, he believed he had uncovered serious weaknesses in their computer systems. He hoped the companies would pay for his recently acquired knowledge.

Klein and the personnel officer chatted as they waited for the others to arrive. The minutes passed. The conversation

1

turned from pleasantries to computer security. The personnel officer suggested Klein's methods might have broken the law. A telephone rang and the personnel officer answered. He said it was a colleague who would be with them shortly. They continued talking.

Twenty minutes later the door opened and a second executive walked in. Suddenly, pushing in behind him, five more men barged into the room. Two of them pulled back their jacket lapels, displaying shoulder holsters and pistols. Klein was too surprised to move. The first two men, Larry Amaker and Dennis Letts, announced that they worked for the Secret Service, the US Treasury's fraud-investigation and intelligence section. They told Klein a hidden video camera had recorded all their conversations. The friendly business atmosphere evaporated.

Klein was arrested, read his rights and questioned for twenty-five minutes before being taken to the Secret Service's offices in Philadelphia. The rest of the day he was held and questioned repeatedly about his hacking activities. Agents went to his home, where they seized papers and print-outs. A state attorney was brought in and Klein was released on bail of $10,000, on condition that he would not leave the tristate area of New York, Pennsylvania and New Jersey. He was told he was being investigated for extortion and interstate racketeering.

'I was so scared. I didn't know what the hell was going on,' Klein said later. 'They grabbed me and held me. They wanted to scare me. Your future looks a little bleak when they threaten you with life imprisonment if you don't co-operate. But Amaker and Letts . . . it was so professionally handled, the acting talent of those guys.'

Guildford, Surrey: 9 October 1988.

Illuminated by brilliant neon lights, Surrey University's computer room was all but deserted. One last Sunday-evening programmer remained, preoccupied, at his terminal. Edward

BEATING THE SYSTEM

Austin Singh, a twenty-three-year-old former computer student, had been bent over the screen in a corner of the room for five hours. Earlier that evening he had browsed through computer files on a military network in the United States. Now, connected up to a system in Germany, he was absorbed in reading mail left for him on a bulletin board by a colleague in the northeast of England. The focus of his attention was several hundred miles away as he typed instructions into the keyboard.

At 7.10 pm the heavy swing doors behind him were pushed open. Singh turned round. Two men entered. As they approached he had a premonition of what was going to happen. Detective Superintendent Graham Seaby and Detective Inspector Larry Henson of Scotland Yard's Serious Crimes Squad walked up to Singh's desk and sat down on either side of him. 'You shouldn't be here, should you?' Seaby said, passing across his police identification card. 'No,' Singh admitted quietly. As the door swung back, Singh noticed several uniformed university security officers standing outside.

The two detectives asked him to demonstrate what he was doing on the computer system in Germany. He explained that he was connected to it via a computer in America, his satellite link crossing and recrossing the Atlantic. They watched, and then told him he was being arrested on suspicion of burglary.

Despite his protests, he was gripped firmly by Henson and marched out to a police car parked by the University security offices. 'Edward, you have been busted,' Singh kept repeating to himself during the drive to Guildford police station. Locked in a cell, he demanded a pen and paper so that he could take notes. During the next four hours he underwent two interviews. The first one, lasting forty minutes, established who he was and that he did not have permission to be in the University. Later he was questioned about the computer systems he had broken into and how he had gained access to them. He agreed to hand over his computer print-outs, notes and documents.

Around midnight, Singh and the detectives, armed with a

search warrant, left the police station and drove to his mother's house in Leatherhead. Stacked up inside a light-blue GPO box were records nearly a foot thick of his hacking activity. The folded computer print-outs and files were covered in places with scribbled notes, codenames and passwords. The information represented the accumulated intelligence of three years' dedicated, and at times obsessive, computer network research. In the early hours of Monday morning they loaded the paperwork into the back of a police car and returned to Guildford. Henson eagerly searched through the print-outs. He asked Singh where he could find his notes on the electronic fund transfer system of a bank in California which had been penetrated.

Back at the police station Singh was told he was being bailed for a month pending further enquiries. Seaby and Henson left the station after 1 am. Later that morning Singh was released. 'They let me go in the middle of the night,' he recalled later. He had hoped to be driven home. 'But one of the officers said, "We're not a taxi service", so I had to walk the twelve miles back to Leatherhead along the roads.' As he headed home through the damp Surrey lanes his mind kept turning over events, examining his predicament. He felt guilty for telling the police so much. 'On the way back a police car stopped me and asked what I was doing walking along the road at that time in the morning.'

West Berlin, 2 March 1989.

Beside the restored Reichstag building, the Berlin Wall in early 1989 was covered in spray paint graffiti demanding independence for Latvia, Lithuania and Estonia. One slogan read: 'The Party's Over'. Standing on the wooden observation platforms in the West tourists could peer over the Wall. On the far side, beyond a sterile security zone of barbed wire and watchtowers, blocks of flats rose up from the streets of East Berlin.

The same concrete towers could be seen from the open-air

walkway outside Hans Hübner's flat above a co-operative supermarket in the West. In the building's dim stairwell and lift more graffiti decorated the walls: '*Turken Raus*', 'Don't Worry, Be Happy', and the telephone numbers of local girls were scratched into the flaking paint.

Hübner was just considering getting up at 8 am on the Thursday morning as police and intelligence officers mounted the gloomy stairs to his flat. They knocked and demanded to be let in. Once inside they found a computer terminal placed on a desk by the window. Hübner's bed, its legs removed, was against the wall, wedged between boxes full of records. A large, cardboard cartoon cutout of a punk penguin stood below the window. In appearance it was a normal student's flat.

Elsewhere in West Germany that morning, Staatschutz officers carried out raids on twenty computer hackers and their alleged controllers suspected of spying for the East. Officers searched Hübner's flat, the office where the twenty-year-old worked as a computer consultant, and the premises of a former employer. He was taken to the Polizei Praesidium, the police headquarters at Tempelhof in West Berlin. 'The building is beside the airport,' Hübner remarked later. 'It was built by the Nazis in the 1930s. The police had a computer specialist, but he didn't know anything. He just searched through the machine where I hadn't kept anything.'

Hübner was questioned about contacts he had made with a Russian trade official in East Berlin three years before, when he was seventeen. He was told that the investigation into his links with a foreign secret service would continue. At 4 pm, as the light was beginning to fade from the March sky, he was released onto the streets of Berlin – an early exponent of an unappreciated form of electronic *glasnost*.

I

WIRING UP THE GLOBAL VILLAGE

The hacker is at once an explorer, an investigator, a trespasser and a nuisance. He or she may develop into a voyeur, a burglar, a vandal, a spy or an exposer of errors. There is nothing new in these occupations. However, because they are carried out within the context of expanding electronic networks, which are not well understood by a largely technophobic population, the hacker has emerged as a mysterious and powerful figure, a latterday sorcerer who arouses fear and loathing as well as admiration and awe.

Hackers disguise their identities by means of exotic or improbable *noms de guerre*, thought up in the way others might invent catchy titles for new rock bands. The anonymity provides some protection against being traced, helping them to avoid the growing hazards of computer and data-protection laws around the world.

Those who have been arrested have found themselves the subject of intense public curiosity. In a society which is just beginning to realise how dependent on computers it has become, hackers have on occasion been treated as dangerous public enemies. In the US Kevin Mitnick, a computer programmer whose codename was 'Condor', was refused bail, put in solitary confinement and only allowed use of a prison telephone under supervision. The authorities in Los Angeles, made nervous by reports of his hacking prowess and interference with telephone lines, feared any contact he might have with electronic networks.

Only within the last few years has the word hacker been defined as someone who penetrates the computer systems of others. For the previous two decades the term was used to describe enthusiastic computer developers who pushed back the boundaries of hardware and software engineering. The Silicon Valley pioneers who devised personal computers thought of themselves as hackers. Their aim was to create new applications for computer technology, rather than puzzling out how to gain access to other people's mainframe systems. Most of those involved on the West Coast in the 1960s and 1970s would dispute the modern definition of the hacker as too narrow and negative.

The two definitions are not entirely at odds with one another, however. Both types of hackers share a fascination, if not an obsession, with computer programming. The best modern hackers are those who understand a variety of computer languages, are conversant with the intricacies of many commercial operating systems, and inventive enough to devise further programs to outwit existing security devices. In many cases young, amateur hackers have gone on to become experienced program writers, realising the value of their expertise in the marketplace.

Hacking has, on occasions, exposed the glib sales patter of computer multinationals to ridicule. If hackers had not uncovered flaws in computer networks, many improvements in the design of information technology might never have been implemented. 'Power to the Networkers', one computer company poster declared in 1989. But hacking has challenged the commercial dream of creating a global village by electronic networks, and has forced the multinationals to reassess the

8

design of open-access systems and devise new security measures. The international network community has created its own social problems.

Charles Babbage, the nineteenth-century English mathematician, was arguably the first hacker, using the term in its earlier computer sense. He devised principles and constructed working models which were later accepted as forerunners of the modern computing machines. Babbage set out a series of definitions of a machine which would take the drudgery out of mathematical calculation and eventually, he hoped, improve on human accuracy. His work was encouraged and supported by Lady Ada Lovelace, Byron's daughter and a contemporary mathematician often described as the world's first programmer. (As a tribute to her, the name Ada was later used for a defence computer programming language developed in the 1960s.)

In 1822 he constructed a prototype – the Difference Engine – which he believed would help actuaries calculate life expectancy and sailors refine navigational charts. Work on a later, larger machine, for which he received several thousand pounds' support from the government of the day, was halted in 1836 when Whitehall cut off further funds. The Analytical Engine went no further than the drawing board. Since then it has been argued that it failed merely because the right components were not available. Babbage's concepts exerted a powerful influence on the direction of research in the century that followed, but few now consider his Analytical Engine to be the theoretical model of the metallic monsters that were assembled in the 1940s, machines we recognise today as the first real computers. The Science Museum in South Kensington is now engaged in reconstructing Babbage's Difference Engine in an attempt to evaluate its performance. It is due to be completed by 1991, the bicentenary of Babbage's birth.

Most contemporary computers are based on the serial design developed by, among others, the Hungarian mathematician John von Neumann shortly after the Second World War. Neumann, who went to lecture at Princeton in 1930, eventually helped to develop high-speed digital computers as well as working on the design of the American atomic and hydrogen bombs. His scheme envisaged calculations being carried out in series, one after another. Although by the 1950s computers were being dubbed 'electronic brains', their functions were far simpler than those of the human mind, which is capable of carrying out a multitude of operations simultaneously – what has come to be known as parallel processing.

Modern conventional computer architecture, which still relies on the designs outlined by von Neumann, contains a number of basic functions: a central processor, a memory, an arithmetic unit similar to an abacus, and an input/output device. These internal structures are likely to be replaced eventually by parallel processing. Neural computing, which imitates the more complex functioning of the human brain, may supersede both. The first generation of computers, designed in the 1940s, operated on electronic vacuum tubes. The second used transistor-based technology. The third generation relied on integrated circuits, also known as chips. The fourth generation is now attempting to squeeze more and more circuitry onto each chip.

In the same way that a simplistic description of a human might split the whole into the mind and body, computers are commonly divided into hardware and software. The hardware is the electronic chips and circuitry, the software the programs and electronic impulses which travel along the system's pathways and circuits. The interface between the hardware and software is conducted in machine code, electrical impulses based on a binary system which are received by the machine's memory unit.

Above the level of the fundamental instructions set into the chip is the operating system in the software. This is the internal communications structure which recognises and carries out instructions. It is sometimes written in machine code or assembly language, but more generally in higher-level computer languages. Among the more widely used operating systems are: MS-DOS and PC-DOS (written by the US firm Microsoft) and CP/M (from Digital Research), all of which are used on personal computers; VMS (from Digital Equipment), used on mid-range computers; MVS or VM, used on the majority of IBM mainframes; Primos, used on Prime computers; and Unix.

Unix is rapidly becoming the standard international operating system for all levels of computers in both the scientific and the commercial worlds. Although developed by one company – AT&T – it has been enhanced and supported by a wide range of computer manufacturers and research institutions. There are now numerous varieties of Unix, chiefly divided into two rival camps, though all share the ultimate aim of creating a common operating system which can be transferred from one machine to another. This will permit users to shop around for the cheapest hardware without losing their investment in software programs, which can be the most expensive part of a system. Most machines communicate with one another at operating systems level. Most hackers specialise in one operating system or another, arguing about which are the easiest to penetrate and manipulate.

Above the level of the operating system are the application programs. They can be as simple as word processing, payroll or accountancy packages, or sophisticated enough to simulate accidents or control space flight. Scientists from the Atomic Energy Authority at Harwell, for example, helped discover the cause of the King's Cross tube disaster in 1987 by simulating the fire with the help of a three-dimensional graphics program on a Cray supercomputer.

That many different proprietary computers can now be linked to one another and communicate without the need for complex software-translation programs is partially thanks to the Open

Systems Interconnection movement, known as OSI. Its proponents have encountered serious resistance from manufacturers who prefer to tie their customers to their own brand of equipment. But users have fought back and demanded that the industry consider their interests. Rival mainframe manufacturers have enabled users to outflank the larger computer corporations by producing cheaper and compatible machines. This has affected IBM in particular, which has been faced with a large number of imitators. They are often referred to as 'plug compatible' companies and include firms such as Amdahl, NAS, Hitachi and Fujitsu. The same development has occurred in the field of personal computers, where imitations of IBM machines are referred to as 'clones'.

For Big Blue, as IBM is known because of its size and the colour of its older mainframe computers, the competition has had its compensations in the form of licence fees and the sale of proprietary software to the users of plug compatible machines. Manufacturers have had to face the fact that they will lose clients if they do not provide them with the means of linking their equipment to that of rival producers. To improve compatibility, most manufacturers now accept the need to be involved with standards-making bodies. Attempts to develop standards to which all the warring factions will eventually agree can last for months or years. With individual manufacturers keen to protect their interests, the process can sometimes resemble peace negotiations over the Middle East. In some cases a standard is agreed only to be swiftly rendered inadequate by fresh technological innovations.

It is with the evolution of networked computing that the hacker has been provided with the means of travelling around the world electronically, hopping from machine to machine. The first computers were giant, number-crunching mainframes developed by companies like IBM, the largest computer company in the world, Univac (now Unisys), and Honeywell (now

Bull). These were 'stand-alone' machines linked to nothing else, ensuring that the information in them was secure from all except those who physically obtained access to the room where the computer was situated. The remote user simply did not exist.

But companies began to realise that stand-alones were uneconomic and began connecting up networks of mainframes so that data could be shared between different sites. Distributed computing (localised networks) was born with the development of the first minicomputers – the range of machines between mainframes and personal computers. Computing mythology has it that Digital Equipment (now the second largest international computer manufacturer) took the name from the miniskirts of the 1960s. Digital's official name for its first commercial minicomputer was rather less glamorous: the 'PDP-5'.

Where early mainframe computers took up entire floors of a building, minicomputers were a more manageable size, as well as being cheaper. Users then gradually realised that they needed to link up these machines not only within one building or site but to other sites across the country and, eventually, if they had foreign subsidiaries, to others abroad. To achieve full and efficient use of the expensive technology, as many users within a company as possible were provided with access.

Networking began to realise its full potential in the 1980s with the growth of packet switching and the rapid proliferation of personal computers – pcs – which placed the power to compute onto everyone's desktop, and multiplied the number of points of access to any computer site. While the flexibility of allowing many users to share computing resources increased commercial efficiency, it also weakened a system's security.

Computer networks have become playgrounds for hackers. As each day passes, the networks become more extensive and interconnected. Some are linked by normal telephone lines. Others operate on dedicated public or private data lines.

Data can be sent around the world in the same way that a

voice can be transmitted through a telephone network, that is by land line, satellite, microwaves, radio or optical fibre. Rather than having a line for each connection, telephone systems use switches which bring all the signals into a common point before sending them off to their specified destination.

The first automatic switch was invented in 1889 by Almon Strowger, a Kansas City undertaker. To his annoyance his local telephone switchboard operator was married to a rival undertaker. Whenever she received calls requesting to be connected to Strowger's funeral parlour she diverted them to her husband's business instead. Despairing at the loss of custom, Strowger spent two years working on an automatic switching device that would render the operator redundant by connecting calls directly to the dialled number. His device was so successful that Strowger switching systems are still in use all over the world. Later versions relied on electrical switching.

In Britain, British Telecom is in the process of replacing mechanical and electrical switches with digital exchanges operating on computer software. These have enabled the faster transmission of data by using packet switching. This method assembles groups of up to 128 characters in 'packets'. Each packet has its address attached to its head and is then despatched. The network will switch it through to its final destination by the most efficient route possible. Data lines are cheaper than voice lines because they operate on a simpler digital on/off sequence and on a narrower frequency range than speech. Packet switching enables many users to 'share a common highway', as Chris Buckley, a leading British networks expert, explains: 'It's much cheaper to put passengers in carriages rather than give them one train each. With packet switching you can combine low-use terminals with high-use lines.'

In Britain the main public data network, which is run by British Telecom, is called Packet Switch Stream (PSS). It conforms to the international X.25 telecommunications standard for data transmission developed at the National Physical Laboratory in

Teddington, near London. In America the equivalent public data networks are Telenet and Tymnet (which British Telecom has recently bought).

Semi-public data networks, based on the need for universities, research institutions and private companies to exchange scientific information, have both expanded and become more formalised over the years. In the US the most extensive is Arpanet, known also as Internet. Arpanet stands for Advanced Research Projects Agency and is owned by the US Government. Internet stands for International Net, because it has grown so far.

A number of more specialised networks have evolved, particularly in the States where most have gateways into Arpanet. Among those most enthusiastically explored by hackers are Milnet, which connects up American military installations, research centres and arms manufacturers, and SPAN, the Space Physics Analysis Network. Milnet was separated from Arpanet in 1983 because of fear of penetration by hackers, but it could still be reached, for example, through an outdialler from Arpanet. The required numbers were widely circulated amongst hackers.

In Britain, Janet (the Joint Academic Network) links up between eighty and ninety universities and polytechnics. It has gateways onto PSS and through to other networks, including Arpanet. It also has direct links to research centres around the world. Many hackers in the United Kingdom gained their first knowledge of computer systems and networks on Janet when they were at college and had hours of spare time each week. Computer networks within academic environments are designed to be relatively open so that research scientists can easily gain access to data on experiments or publications. It is an ideal training ground for the dedicated hacker to learn the geography of the networks and the finer points of a wide variety of operating systems. It is also a rich hunting ground for esoteric research centres and forbidden secrets; a number of universities participate in military research, such as the Star Wars

(SDI) projects. In late 1988 Janet's administrators decided to introduce tougher security measures onto the network because it was becoming such a well-known target for hackers. These measures, it was claimed, meant offenders could be traced back to local areas and sometimes to individual phone numbers or accounts.

Alongside the expansion of public and research networks has been the growth of private networks run by security-conscious organisations such as defence contractors, military establishments and financial institutions. Some have links to public networks, others operate in isolation. Many use a mixture of the two and pay for them to be managed by either the public network suppliers, for example British Telecom or Mercury in Britain, or by one of a handful of specialist computer network suppliers, such as EDS (part of General Motors), Fastrak (a subsidiary of the Midland Bank), or Istel (formerly a division of British Leyland and now owned by the American company AT&T). Digital of Massachusetts boasts in its advertising handouts that it has the largest private or corporate network in the world, with 30,000 distributed systems connected to it.

The result of this international sprawl of interlinking chains of communications is a web of networks far too elaborate and extensive to illustrate in a single diagram. It is a web which is expanding all the time. Using international telephone lines, links to the Eastern bloc have been possible for some time. Several years ago, for example, hackers in Hamburg set up connections to some of the few computer enthusiasts in East Germany to relay information on common environmental issues such as the pollution of the River Elbe.

In early 1989, a satellite network link connecting systems in California and Moscow was established. The San Francisco–Moscow Teleport was supported, with reservations, by both Soviet and American Governments. Both sides are able to monitor its activities. The US Department of Defense was particularly concerned about the transfer of electronics technology to the East, much of which, it believes, has potential military applications. The Teleport, which can communicate voice, data and visual information, has been widely used by scientists, American businesses eager to contact a growing number of subsidiaries in the Soviet Union, and computer enthusiasts hoping to meet counterparts in the USSR. The Soviet Union end of the link is controlled by the Institute for Automated Systems in Moscow. 'We do not foresee any political or social obstacles to the smooth increase of two-way electronic communications between our two countries. We are witnessing a great demand for such a service in our country and abroad,' Oleg Smirnov, the director of the Institute, told the *New York Times* in February 1989.

The number of personal computers in the Soviet Union is still small. In late 1989 it was estimated at only 200,000 Western-compatible pcs in a population of 270 million; at the same time, one in eight people in the United States owned a pc. Computing is an exclusive pastime in the USSR. For a long time any Russian wishing to keep a computer had to demonstrate a good reason to the authorities for having it at home. The situation, however, is changing. A meeting in Moscow in December 1988 founded the International Computer Club which intends to organise exchanges between Russian and American computer students. *Newsweek* reported in March 1989 that a young Soviet programmer, Alexei Pazhitnov, sold 100,000 copies of the computer game he had written to Americans. The British telecommunications company, GPT, is in the process of negotiating the sale of System X digital telephone exchanges to Moscow. In September 1989 a Californian computer company, Phoenix Group International, signed a joint-venture deal to provide three million personal computers to Soviet schools and universities by 1994. Once the technological infrastructure for networks has been established, hacking is likely to follow.

The Californian–Soviet joint venture, dubbed Samcom, was made possible only by the relaxation of high-technology export restrictions earlier that year. Over the last two decades, as the gap between the West's and the East's electronic development has widened, the Soviets have been evermore eager to obtain technology from abroad. Their enthusiasm has been matched by US Government determination to prevent them from doing so. The result was the creation of Cocom, the Co-ordinating Committee for Multilateral Export Controls. Its headquarters are in Paris and its members include NATO's fifteen participating countries, plus Japan. Cocom committees meet weekly, monitor all technology deals with the Communist bloc, and draw up lists of prohibited and permitted goods. In Britain, Cocom's regulations are enforced under the Customs and Excise Management Act.

Margaret Thatcher has supported Cocom's work enthusiastically. In 1983 a special committee was set up to coordinate the work of Customs and Excise officers, the Foreign Office and the intelligence services in tracking down illegal exports. Over the years there have been a number of prosecutions of British businessmen. In 1986 a computer engineer was sentenced at Bristol Crown Court to nine months in prison for shipping advanced electronic equipment to Moscow. Later that year, a west London businessman was jailed for a year for shipping equipment, including integrated printed circuits, to Poland, Hungary and Czechoslovakia. A senior Pentagon official flew to Britain in 1987 to give evidence on the potential military uses of smuggled equipment in the case of a Chelmsford businessman convicted of sending proscribed equipment to the Communist bloc.

In the early 1980s the sale of computerised machine tools by Toshiba to a Leningrad shipyard prompted US defence officials to claim it would take years for the West to regain the lead in underwater technology. The £10 million worth of equipment, it was alleged, helped the Soviet Navy reduce propeller noise in submarines. Toshiba Machinery, a subsidiary of the main company, was eventually fined £8,000 in a Tokyo court in 1988.

Toshiba itself was banned from selling consumer products at American military bases.

Even with the arrival of *glasnost*, Cocom officials have shown little initial desire to loosen restrictions. An American official told *Computing* magazine in early 1989: 'There has been the Gorbachev reform and certainly a change of tone in the East, but as far as the US is concerned we don't feel that anything has happened thus far that would justify us letting our guard down in the military field or in the Cocom field. The Soviet Union is continuing to steal or get this critical Western technology by one illegal means or another.'

Mr Gorbachev has personally shown a strong interest in Western technology, especially for civilian applications, seeing it as a vital ingredient in his restructuring of the sluggish Soviet economy. On one brief visit to Britain in April 1988, he squeezed in a visit to Case, a Hertfordshire communications company already involved in export deals with Moscow. Gorbachev has also expressed strong views on the West's technology embargoes. In his book *Perestroika*, published in the UK, the Soviet leader alleged that the American tactics were not only directed against the Soviet Union but also at other 'rival non-American firms'. He added: 'Every cloud has a silver lining. We have drawn lessons from the decisions taken by the US and some other Western countries to refuse to sell the Soviet Union advanced technology. That is perhaps why we are now experiencing a real boom in the fields of information science, computer technology and other areas of science and technology.'

Mistrust of America's championing of the Cocom rules is not limited to the Eastern bloc. There have been many internal political rows over the list of sanctions. The West German Foreign Minister, Hans-Dietrich Genscher, described much of the technology banned from export as being 'out of date' and the whole notion as a reflection of outmoded Cold War thinking. Many of the embargoed goods represent no threat to Western security. In Britain there has been widespread dissatisfaction with Cocom among businessmen who find the regulations labyrinthine and oppressive. Some American high-technology sales to the UK are only allowed under licence, with no re-export permitted unless a further licence is obtained. In November 1988, *Despatches*, the Channel Four current affairs programme, claimed that Cocom was an elaborate attempt to block European computer sales to the East while helping American companies to find markets, under licence, in the Communist bloc. Between 1982 and 1986 British sales rose from $23.4 million to only $24.7 million, while US sales to the East increased over tenfold, from $228 million to $3.6 billion over the same period.

This argument was highlighted by the controversial British case of Brian Butcher, who was lured to Italy and arrested there by the American FBI and local police. British Customs had refused to help the American authorities because the offences with which Butcher was later charged were not extraditable in the UK. Held in an Italian jail for two months, Butcher was flown to the States where he was tried on five counts of breaching export controls. The allegations related to importing second-hand computers to Britain for re-export. Eventually he was fined £15,000 and his case was taken up by MPs at Westminster, Paddy Ashdown among them. Speaking from inside his American jail, Butcher warned: 'One day everybody is going to wake up and find that all the electronics industry [in Britain] is finished and we will be totally reliant on America for everything and, of course . . . that is what the big American firms want.'

In the summer of 1989, Cocom did announce an extensive relaxation of restrictions on the sale of many types of personal computer. Personal computers modelled on the IBM range could now be sold in the East, but embargoes were left in force on larger computers – restrictions that still anger European and American companies.

II

HOW TO HACK

'My grandmother could do it' – Edward Austin Singh

Towards the end of 1988, Transworld Airlines' London office was forced to overhaul its Freefone telephone answering service after it had been alerted to its abuse by gangs of telephone phreakers. To 'phreak' is to make telephone calls for free and there is no better target than a faulty 0800 Freefone telephone line which saves the phreaker the cost of even a local telephone call. In TWA's case, once the taped message ended, the phreaker, hearing a new dialling tone, would redial using an outside-call prefix number, and then make calls all over the world, leaving TWA to foot the bill. Although TWA said it noticed little difference in its bill, just to be sure it called in British Telecom who put an inhibitor on the line to prevent further abuse.

Phreaking is a precursor of hacking, dating from the 1950s when international direct dialling was introduced in the US. It became popular to try to get a free ride off the telephone company, which was believed to be making exorbitant profits. Computer hackers often employ phreaking skills because the most important tool of their trade is the telephone line and

21

many cannot afford to pay the vast telephone bills they run up. Some hackers make use of firms having faults with the call diverters that automatically reroute calls to staff out of hours. The caller pretends to have the wrong number and when the recipient hangs up he finds himself still connected to an open line. This enables him to ring out for free.

Mercury, the number two in Britain's telecommunications duopoly, has had its problems too. In spring 1989 it emerged that enthusiasts were circulating details about the best way to phreak Mercury telephone networks and land subscribers with the bill. Mercury phones are programmed with individual user codes which are based on electronic tones identifying each subscriber. This should keep them secure – as long as the user codes do not fall into the wrong hands. Mercury said the claims were exaggerated. Only the company's early model of telephone was at risk, of which there were barely thirty left in circulation at the end of 1989. 'It was possible that a personal identification number could be listened for in the early phones, but a person would have to put a listening device on the phone and to do that they would have to get in to the user's premises,' a company official explained. 'Devices have been added to subsequent telephones to protect them – although there are those who say anything is possible for someone sufficiently numerate in computers.'

Phreaking in the UK has not taken on the same epidemic proportions as in the US, where in the 1970s the self-proclaimed Youth International Party Line (YIPL) set up with the intention of trying to reduce profits for 'Ma Bell' (the AT&T Bell Corporation), which was then a single company, but is now broken up into several smaller Bell operating companies. YIPL believed it was a 'fascist' and capitalistic organisation whose influence needed to be stemmed: 'YIPL is an anti-profit organisation dedicated to people's technology, and we publish information that shows you how to fight back at the computers that run our lives,' the group's newsletters stated. Advice to subscribers, who paid $4 a year if they could afford it ('If you're poor and can't afford it, it's free'), included how to phreak more efficiently and, with detailed hand-drawn diagrams, how to build phreaking devices – blue, red or black boxes. These were also known as 'organs' or tone generators, which when attached to phones could generate signals to match the frequencies used to connect calls.

Some of YIPL's advice was less conventional. The February 1972 issue suggested which brass washers were best for coin boxes and how to go about getting them. 'Some [stores] will refuse to sell [washers] to phreaks, so have your respectable friends go in and play plumber or call in orders and then play messenger,' the magazine suggested. One reader wrote in with the suggestion: 'A very good way to obtain extra phones is to get them out of empty apartments from non-phreek [the spelling of phreak is as varied as its methods] friends who have had their phones disconnected but not removed . . . Ma Bell doesn't remove phones from empty apartments until new tenants move in.' Later that year, the group began a campaign to 'Support Cap'n Crunch', America's legendary phreaker, who was arrested in 1971 for abusing the telephone system. Readers were asked to contribute what they could to the cause, with the sobering reminder, 'It might be you next.'

Cap'n Crunch (aka John Draper) had become infamous for phreaking with the aid of a whistle given away free with packets of Cap'n Crunch breakfast cereal. Blowing through the whistle into the mouthpiece, Draper found he could generate the 2,600 hertz tone of the telephone system, thereby enabling him to make free telephone calls. In the early 1970s Draper helped Steve Jobs and Steve Wozniak (who later founded Apple Computers) design blue boxes. Draper – a successful software consultant despite his past convictions for joy-riding on the telephone system – now makes celebrity appearances at hacking forums around the world.

Draper's case raised public awareness of phreaking, although the first 'blue box' had been confiscated in the US in a police raid as early as 1961. Among those involved in phreaking early on in Britain was the investigative reporter, Duncan Campbell. He covered the subject extensively for *New Scientist* in the early 1970s, writing in part on the basis of his own experience. Campbell's later technological interests, to the annoyance of the authorities, have included MI5's and GCHQ's computers, as well as government spy satellites.

For the computer hacker whistles and blue boxes are only occasional tools. More essential are a computer, a telephone, and a modem (modulator/demodulator). A modem converts signals for transmission and reception across the telephone line. It enables home-computer enthusiasts anywhere to link up with networks around the world, and to vary the speed with which their computers talk to other computers. With these the hacker has the means to enter the expanding world of computer networks. If he wants to keep a record of his activities, then he can add a printer to his toolkit. Almost any home computer can be used to hack, from an Amstrad PCW to a BBC micro, Amiga or Commodore 64. Even a small Tandy laptop computer can be used. For machines that do not have built-in modems, all that is required is a serial port – a slot in the back of the computer to plug in the modem – and a terminal emulation software package to enable the computer to communicate with the outside world.

Experienced hackers tend to use more upmarket machines than home computers. They recommend business personal computers such as Apple Macintoshes or IBM Personal Computers and their 'clones'. Business machines generally have better definition screens and can display eighty characters to a line. Basic home computers, such as those built for playing space invaders, display only forty characters. This is important for the serious hacker because larger systems – the usual target of a hack – almost always use eighty-character screens. If a hacker has little patience it is best to buy an expensive modem which will send and receive data quickly. But if he is strapped for cash then a cheap one will do. It is possible to pick one up from a local computer shop for under £50. A well-off computer enthusiast will go for something in the region of several hundred pounds, but the average hacker will probably own one worth nearer £100. The slowest of any practical use is a 300-baud modem which can carry thirty characters a second. A more normal speed for Britain is the 1,200-baud duplex, which lets you see two lines of data a second. Duplex means you send and receive data at the same time. Faster speeds available are 2,400 and 4,800.

Most people come in contact with modems, which resemble large, flat shortbread tins, if they use long-distance information retrieval systems, such as Prestel, or have electronic mail systems such as Telecom Gold (both supplied by British Telecom), or any of the various information systems used by businesses such as Reuters, Lexis, Textline, McCarthy Online or Extel. In Britain there are no restrictions on the use of modems. Elsewhere the rules are sometimes more strict. In Germany, where users must obtain a licence to connect anything, including a telephone answering machine, to the telephone line, hackers have been fined for ignoring the law.

Hackers need more than just the kit to succeed. They need to build up, either in a notebook or on computer, a personal data base of practical and technical information, which takes time, and above all, patience. The most useful information to get hold of in the beginning is a list of network user addresses (NUAs). These are the computer world's equivalent of telephone numbers and are, in some cases, easily available. In fact many organisations allow their numbers to be published, because they wish their customers to be able to find them easily in the public network. If you have a legitimate PSS account (obtainable for a small initial down payment), then you will receive a directory of addresses automatically. PSS has over 100,000 users making one million calls a day. British Telecom admits that there are security risks in publishing these numbers, but maintains that only information-providing services are listed in the directory. Those systems, like many others, are programmed only to accept authorised callers.

A more popular method of obtaining network addresses and passwords is to log on to one of the many hundreds of bulletin boards that sit on networks or are accessible through telephone lines all over the world. Bulletin board systems (BBSs) are, in effect, electronic wallposters. They are usually run on a personal computer belonging to an enthusiast. The first bulletin boards took off in the early 1980s when the pc boom began; others exist in the unused parts of commercial mainframes or minicomputers connected to public networks.

Users access the bulletin board by dialling up over the public switched telephone network. Specialist pc publications, such as *Personal Computer World* and *Personal Computer Magazine*, and manufacturer specific magazines such as *MacUser*, publish lists of bulletin board numbers for the enthusiast. Often, groups of users of a particular make of computer will have their own bulletin board for exchanging advice on how to get round technical problems in their system's hardware or software. Computer companies also run them as helplines for users who have problems with their software.

The programming enthusiast will exchange his software programs over the bulletin board. 'Shareware' is also attracting a large degree of interest amongst computer users. For a small subscription fee – at present £35 a year – they can have access to certain bulletin boards which allow them to download onto their own computers – free of charge – one-off specialist programs written by enthusiasts. Some bulletin boards are 'read-only' and not interactive, meaning they cannot talk back to an individual user. An example of this is one run by the US Department of Commerce. It provides statistical information on the different US federal agencies, important dates and future products and services. Users pay a small fee each year to have access to it.

There are at least 200 private bulletin boards on computers based in Britain and there are many thousands more worldwide. In a few cases companies choose not to discourage bulletin boards set up on their systems because they see hacking as a useful test of their software. Among these was Shox, a bulletin board and chat system on Altger, one of the most popular hacker bulletin boards in Europe. (A chat system allows users to converse, but nothing is stored for later retrieval.) Altger is a Unix machine belonging to the German office of the US computer manufacturer, Altos. The main bulletin board was closed down in 1987, but its chat system remains a favourite amongst members of the German hacker group, Chaos, and is also frequented by British, American and other European hackers. Singh described Altger as the main trading point for passwords, with up to thirty hackers chatting on line at one time. It was similar to Citizens Band radio, with callers using the term 'hacking handle' to describe their pseudonyms. If Singh encountered difficulties in reaching his target during a hack, he would call up the Altos machine to ask fellow board users for help with passwords or technical information.

(Altos was well aware of the hacking activity going on in its machines; its chat system was open to anyone. The company's systems support manager in Munich, Michael Hentricht, noted that Italian hackers exchanged the most passwords. The fact that hackers use the system does not bother him. 'If it did I would cut it off,' he said. 'We don't close it because often the German authorities – the federal police – come to our offices when they are hunting for a hacker. They came last autumn and found clues for their inquiry into the KGB hackers. Some of those arrested had been using our computers.' Altos does run a quasi-bulletin board for 400 authorised users to swap information on Unix. Hentricht claims it is almost impossible for hackers to break into these sections now. Previous attempts have shown him where the holes are in the system and he has managed to close them. For this reason he is quite in favour of playing host to hackers.)

It takes a few weeks for a novice hacker to be accepted by the other members of the community, but eventually he or she will be helped out and offered a network address or password to launch a hack. After six or eight weeks of persistent attempts, the hacker will have at least one fairly decent password to exchange. The game escalates from there. When hacking took off in the early 1980s, passwords and addresses were readily exchanged. This camaraderie tailed off a few years ago when experienced hackers got tired of giving and getting little in return. Although that situation appears to be relaxing again, with hackers becoming less paranoid and more willing to share their information, the most dedicated hackers attempt to keep certain sections of bulletin boards exclusive by encrypting the information they keep there.

Becoming an accepted user of some of the more secretive bulletin boards can resemble applying for membership of a Masonic lodge. The process can begin with a recommendation from a fellow hacker followed by a telephone or on-line interview with its operators who then will decide what security level to give the applicant. If successful he might have to pay a nominal fee, such as £5, to receive a personal password. If, however, a member breaks the bulletin board's particular code of conduct, the operator might then hold what is known as a teletrial, when the operator interrogates the errant user and if dissatisfied, might remove certain levels of the miscreant's security authorisation or outlaw him alto-gether. Many experienced hackers, who merely want to test the worth of a computer system, are not interested in the more dubious information held on some bulletin boards. Those that seek a challenge greater than swapping passwords across the network often prefer not to use bulletin boards in their quests. 'Bulletin boards are for the nappies,' one hacker said disdainfully.

Most hackers get a foot on the hacking ladder simply by examining publicly available information. For example, there are a small number of technical books on hacking techniques, such as Hugo Cornwall's *Hacker's Handbook*, and many volumes on how different computer operating systems work. The most comprehensive books on operating systems are the manuals which accompany a new system when it is purchased. Such detailed technical information can sometimes also be picked up at computer exhibitions where a good proportion of visitors are not besuited businessmen but rather jeans-clad youngsters carrying plastic bags stuffed full of hand-outs. College libraries are a reasonable source too. Singh spent much of his spare time engrossed in library books covering the finer points of operating systems.

Armed with such intelligence, a hacker can recognise a system as soon as he comes across it on the network. Whether it be based on Unix, Digital Equipment's VMS or IBM's MVS operating system, the hacker will be ready to exploit at speed the knowledge that he has amassed. Operating system manuals are important, not only because the hacker can learn how to use a particular system, but also because they contain system passwords – known as default passwords – which are used to get the software running when it is first installed. Users are meant to change these immediately. They usually do, but many systems administrators forget or cannot be bothered to change them. Although the same password is not used for all deliveries, the same ones keep cropping up. The US computer-maker Prime uses such words as 'system, system'. On other systems, when a field engineer overhauls an installation he might use the IDs *field*, *support*, *test*, *remote* or *user*, plus a password. It is up to the administrator to change it afterwards. He often does not, which makes access easy for the hacker.

BEATING THE SYSTEM

If the systems administrator has been security conscious enough to change either the default passwords or those left by the maintenance engineer, then the hacker has to resort to other methods. The first line of attack is to try out as many common passwords as possible. Few passwords reach even the imaginative heights of 'Open Sesame'. Most users pick common first names, often their own. Other favourites are names of spouses, heroes from history, football, films and the pop world, and words relating to sex. Some people hardly bother to make any effort. David Black, computer audit partner with accountants Spicer and Oppenheim, revealed at a conference on computer security in 1989 that at a particular computer installation which had been warned about using passwords that were too common, sixty-one were AAAAAA, two had been changed to BBBBBB, six passwords were single letters, two were made up of two characters, thirty were first names or nicknames, and thirteen were names of people no longer working there. And, claimed Black, this was a company totally committed to computer security.

If the hacker is too impatient to attempt the direct safe-breaking method of trying every password or combination he can think of, there are other means. As an insider at a company or university, for example, he or she can pick up passwords by 'shoulder-surfing' – literally looking over someone's shoulder to see which keys a user presses when entering a password (it will not show up on the screen). More simply, there will be several users who do not trust their own memory and will write the password on a piece of paper and stick it to their terminals. A more devious form of research is to hunt through rubbish bags which may contain useful computer print-outs or, worse still, search through people's private papers. Another method, but only for the most obsessive hacker, is to gather information by what has been called 'social engineering'. It might better be described as impersonation. This usually means posing as an employee, either by telephone or by entering the premises of a target company, to pick up passwords. Some hackers are more audacious than others: one American hacker claimed to have socially engineered his way in to 30,000 machines.

Kevin Mitnick, the notorious American telephone phreaker, obtained his information by walking in to buildings in disguise or by calling up the systems department and pretending to be a maintenance man. His skills – which had previously included hacking from a public phone box with the help of a portable computer – left him languishing in a US jail in 1989, having been found guilty of causing $4 million worth of damage to Digital systems and copying $1 million worth of the company's software.

Before a password can be used, however, the hacker must know the network user address (NUA), the protocol (an agreed procedure for letting data communicate across different computer systems), the log-on procedure and sometimes the caller's user identity (NUI).

If the hacker has failed to find out any of these, there are other methods of making the connections. Auto-dial programs can be bought to fire out a range of telephone numbers until one hits a modem and allows the hacker's system to make the connection. There are legitimate dictionary computer programs on the market which a clever programmer can adapt and use for finding passwords. The program will run through the dictionary, firing out each word until it comes up with an existing password. Hackers may construct their own short dictionary of common names and favourite passwords. If the password is believed to be a figure, a program can be used which generates many permutations of numbers. Eventually one will be accepted as a genuine password. Hackers call these programs 'scanners' or 'sprinters'. These methods are usually far too time-consuming – setting up each new call can take ten seconds – and, more importantly, their use is severely restricted since after three attempts at a password most systems will drop the line. Although common in hacker mythology, sprinters are of limited use in initially trying to penetrate a system.

Once the hacker has gained access to a system he can try something more advanced by inserting a 'capture' program – also known as a screen-mimic program – into the target terminal. That way, when a legitimate user logs on, first by tapping in his name, then his password, the capture program can scoop up the passwords. The genuine user will think he or she has made an error in logging on, so will try again. In the meantime the capture program will store the ID and passwords. The next time the hacker enters the system he can collect the information stored for him. This enables him to vary his electronic impersonations. The hacker thus obtains the privileges of the user. Capture programs are normally inserted by physically gaining access to a terminal, although they can be placed in systems remotely.

Singh had developed a more sophisticated version of such a capture program, allowing him to capture NUAs, IDs and passwords without gaining access to the system. His capture program managed to intercept network users before they logged on to their target system by emulating the PAD (the Packet Assembler/Disassembler or network node which directs traffic to its final network destination). The program convinced the caller they were being interrogated by the genuine PAD and they typed in their required NUA, ID and passwords. These were then stored in a host system from which they were later retrieved.

Although most computer systems have user IDs and passwords stored in encrypted form in a special file, it is possible to write a decryption program which will unscramble them. The hacker will have to know the encryption algorithm which is stored somewhere within the system. Once they have obtained this, they can encrypt a dictionary or a book of names stored electronically and by a further program compare the encrypted passwords with dictionary words. The program will select those that are the same, revealing matched passwords.

Having obtained access, the next trick is to improve the stolen password's privileges or obtain the systems manager's password by ransacking and later decrypting the password file. This allows the hacker more and more power over the system which has been penetrated. Higher privileges allow access to a greater number of files, files that might be restricted because they contain sensitive personal or financial information. They also grant greater powers in controlling and altering the structure of the system, for example the authority to add or remove user IDs.

When Singh hacked from his hijacked terminal at Surrey University he became expert at jumping from one node (the computer that is linked to the network) to another and from one network to another. He managed this because Surrey University is linked to Janet, which is made up of 400 nodes – and growing by the week. From there, he claimed, he could leap from a Prime computer on the network to one of Prime's own internal company systems. That allowed him to leap across to a Prime system belonging to one of Prime's customers, either in the UK or abroad.

Once into a system, the hacker can plant a back-door program. This usually entails inserting a modification to the log-on authorisation section of the operating system. The back-door circumvents the usual authorisation procedure by allowing the hacker to regain access by using any special password he has planted in the program. Even if a hack is discovered by a systems manager, who then invalidates the original password, the hacker can still gain access unless the original and unaltered authorisation program is reinstalled.

A very astute hacker can also tamper with the auditing program to hide the fact that a back-door has been inserted. Another trick is to make sure that the systems manager is absent from the machine so that whatever is done, is, at least initially, unobserved.

BEATING THE SYSTEM

There are a few hackers who have harmful motives in mind when they break into a system. Such computer vandals use a variety of weapons, the most common of which are 'logic bombs', 'Trojan horses', 'worms' and 'viruses'. These are all self-contained programs which appear to take on lives of their own. In the film *2010*, the sequel to *2001: A Space Odyssey*, scientists on the space mission discover that HAL 9000, the computer that went berserk in the original story, has been infected with a computer tapeworm. (HAL has commonly been thought to denote IBM, since H, A and L are the three letters which alphabetically precede the letters in the corporation's acronym.) The computer-illiterate members of the space crew look perplexed until the computer expert explains that the tapeworm is a program written to perpetuate itself until it has taken up the whole of the computer's memory, confusing HAL to such a degree that it goes 'mad'. Such worms are not programmed to erase or interfere with data but can cause systems to crash by overloading the computing capacity.

By contrast, logic bombs, Trojan horses and viruses are programmed to cause specific damage. All three can remain dormant and harmless until triggered off. The rogue code or program can be activated to be vindictive on a certain date; they can also be just a joke. A Trojan horse, as the name suggests, is hidden within an apparently genuine program. Once activated it can alter data, such as the salaries of certain employees, or transfer money from one bank account to another. The Trojan horse can also be programmed to wipe itself out once it has achieved its objective. Logic bombs are more crude in effect, and are usually designed to crash a system and destroy files. They can be designed to go off on a particular date or when a user keys in a particular word.

The weapon that has caught most people's imaginations is the virus. In the age of AIDS awareness campaigns, the name alone strikes fear into the hearts of computer managers and users. Software companies and user groups advocate safe software practices. The sexual overtones are not entirely flippant since viruses are the most infectious of rogue codes that a computer vandal can plant. They are designed to spread. They have the ability to replicate themselves within a machine and can be transferred from one floppy disc to another and also, but it is less commonplace, across networks of personal computers.

There are a wide variety of virus strains circulating through the computer community at the moment. Some are quite harmless and display amusing messages to users. Others, like worms and logic bombs, can destroy data and wipe clean entire files. The virus threat has increased with the escalation in software piracy – the illegal copying of commercial and private software. Much of this goes on in the underground of the bulletin board world but is also happening in the usually law-abiding field of the corporate user.

UK software suppliers alone lose several hundreds of million pounds in revenue a year because their programs are copied and passed on to other users free of charge. Some companies have even been set up to sell computer hardware which runs pirated software. The Federation Against Software Theft was established in 1984 to try to stamp out piracy. In 1989 a larger international organisation, the Business Software Alliance, was formed by some of the leading software suppliers in the US, including Lotus and Ashton-Tate. It too is trying to win back lost income. Its first raid was in April 1989 against the Italian chemicals company, Montedison, which was accused of using pirated software on its personal computers. The company claimed it had permission to copy the software.

Pirated computer games are often the main carriers of viruses. Employees lend games to colleagues and friends in other companies who make more copies, thus passing the virus on, sometimes into the firm's main system. Viruses have created opportunities for computer consultants who can offer their services in eradicating them from victim systems. In the UK, the British Computer Virus Research Centre and the Computer

Threat Research Association are just two of the organisations set up in the wake of virus publicity to offer advice to the user. Anti-hacking campaigners are particularly anxious to control the advance of viruses, believing they could be used by enemy agents to crash important military computers. The fear is not completely unfounded. Computer software programmed for one of the early space missions to Venus in the 1960s had one piece of punctuation missing. This resulted in NASA losing control of the probe. More recently, in 1988, a Russian unmanned mission to Mars, Phobos I, suffered a breakdown in its on-board computer. In the race to meet the launch timetable, a test program was not removed and a replacement was sent up to the ship after it was launched. According to Martyn Thomas of Praxis Systems, a company specialising in high-integrity software, out of three pages of data dispatched, there was one wrong character. The incorrect program was activated and the Russians lost full control of Phobos I. If a minor slip could create that scale of risk, how many times more dangerous would a premeditated Trojan horse or virus attack be?

When Singh was arrested in Surrey University's computer centre, he joked with journalists that hacking was so simple 'my grandmother could do it'. A throwaway remark, but if any computer-illiterate person with malice in mind was shown a few techniques and handed a file of network addresses, user IDs and passwords, they could be well on their way to wreaking havoc. With a little more time and the help of a virus-writing kit, such as those recently on sale in West Germany, the complete range of the hacker's arsenal could be at their fingertips.

III

THE ELECTRONIC COUNTERCULTURE

Why should anyone wish to spend eight or ten hours alone staring into the pale luminescence of a computer screen? Journalists and typists complain about painful repetitive strain injuries to their wrists induced by hammering away at a terminal's keyboards day after day. North American workforces have insisted their employers provide pregnant women with lead-lined aprons to protect them from low-level radiation given off by the cathode-ray tubes behind computer screens. Trade union negotiators regularly battle with managements over rules permitting staff adequate breaks to avoid eye strain. Indeed a computer, in sales jargon, is often dubbed a 'work station'. The Cyclops-like electronic box squatting on the desk top may make the daily grind marginally less painful, but for most of us it is still a symbol of toil. So how do others overcome terminal boredom?

Straightforward curiosity and a fascination with the intellectual challenge form the most common motivations for hacking. The illicit thrill of outwitting a system's security is compounded by the excitement of realising the potential for future expeditions. Thereafter a strong element of what many describe as addiction is experienced by some young hackers. There is a mesmeric quality about a two-dimensional computer screen which allows a hacker to watch himself circuit the globe electronically. Beyond curiosity there are many reasons for trespassing within the networks, as many as one can dream up uses for the facilities created by or information held on computers. Companionship, career advancement, espionage, criminal fraud, vandalism, political protest, revenge and pure megalomania have all played their part.

Viewed by outsiders, the hacker has been expected to fulfil two crude stereotypes. The first is that he is socially so inadequate he prefers machines to the company of humans, and the second envisages the hacker as all-powerful once seated at the computer terminal. In April 1986, the *Daily Star* ran a front-page story claiming hackers had altered the orbit of a satellite through remote interference with the ground-control computer systems. An alternative role, as embodied in the film *War Games* (1983), casts the hacker in the guise of an electronic rebel taking on the might of the Establishment. The film's teenage hero changes his class grades by hacking into the school computer. He is shown using an automatic password-generating program, and he makes several observations on the state of contemporary computer security, including: 'The more complicated systems are, the more they have to help you', and 'I don't believe any system is totally secure'. He makes reservations for a flight to Paris in order to impress his girlfriend, but admits he can't get the tickets. In the end he uses his home computer to break into a restricted military system and accidentally starts a nuclear war alert.

Within the world of computing professionals, hacking rarely enjoys a glamorous image. Two regular users of the American Government's Advanced Research Projects Agency network (Arpanet) wrote to *The Independent* expressing concern at the potential for damage inherent in electronic networks. Signing themselves JPD and MOBY, they claimed: 'One university in the United States holds an Ugliest Person on Campus contest, which is traditionally won by a computer science student. The "Yah, I'm grotty, I hack and it's fun" ethos probably drives many more of the serious hackers than any thought of stealing 10p from every NatWest account.'

Some would go further. The common view of a computer hacker, according to one British policeman, is of a person who is socially inept, a loner who cannot make his own way in the community. In this view, the hacker, often with a chip on his shoulder, seeks consolation through the impersonality of the computer screen. He has lots of acquaintances through bulletin boards, but rarely meets them. Within this community of electronic identities, the hacker enjoys a position in a defined pecking order. The hierarchy of this international community is established as hackers build up credit through revealing increasingly substantial secrets while swapping information: respect is given to those with the greatest knowledge, those who know best how to beat the system. It is an image of the hacker as an obsessive, clued-up delinquent, a weirdo who poses a danger to society.

A less criminal view is proposed in *The Second Self: Computers and the Human Spirit* written in 1984 by the American sociologist Sherry Turkle. Turkle explores the emerging subculture of hacking at the Massachusetts Institute of Technology. 'In the hacker,' she writes, 'many people see someone who holds a key to the mysteries [of computers] and is willing to defy the Establishment to open them; there is the fantasy of an electronic Robin Hood.' Hackers, she observes, are generally fans of science fiction. But she also comments: 'The hacker culture seems to be made up of people who need to avoid complicated social situations, who for one reason or another got frightened off or hurt too badly by the risks and complexities of relationships.' There are very few women involved. Hackers are not addicted to computer screens, but they sometimes think of sitting at the terminal in terms of getting another fix.

The editor of the 1989 edition of *The Hacker's Handbook*,

Steve Gold, attempted to redress the balance in a lecture on the psychology of hacking at a London computer security conference. He suggested that there was a broader spectrum of personality types involved. 'Hackers are usually intelligent people, their age range is not limited to the adolescent,' he said. 'They are looking for a challenge in life. Often their jobs fail to satisfy this challenge, hence they turn to the computer and its related subject of telecommunications.' He devised four categories for hackers: the beginner, who has no programming ability; the student, who tends to be obsessional and introverted; the mischievous, who is capable of destroying files; and the thief, a rare species who hones his skills for the single purpose of committing fraud via computer.

The growth of groups around the world has led to an increase in the number of terms used to describe hackers. In America they are occasionally 'cyberpunks', a word taken from William Gibson's cult book *Neuromancer*. Dr Timothy Leary, in an interview with *Rolling Stone* magazine, described cyberpunks as 'individuals who have the intelligence and the courage to access and use high-quantum technology for their own purposes and their own modes of communication'. He went on: 'The psychedelic drug movement of the Sixties and the personal computer movement of the Eighties are inner and outer reflections of each other. You simply cannot understand psychedelic drugs, which activate the brain, unless you understand something about computers.'

Other names have also enjoyed some limited currency. In an article in *Computer & Security* magazine, an American security consultant sought to draw a distinction between hacking and cracking. 'Crackers,' the article claimed, 'attempt to compromise the security of systems, whereas hackers merely attempt to understand the technical aspects of systems.' Cracking usually has slightly more destructive connotations. In France the word *piratage* has often been used to describe hacking. More recently, as hacking has increasingly had its reputation blackened by those pressing for legislation in Britain, a Channel Four documentary in late 1989 employed the word 'technopaths' to cover computer enthusiasts whose aim is to cause damage.

Moreover, it is in the nature of computer interaction that games initiated through curiosity can easily shade into more dubious pursuits without the computer user being fully aware of the consequences. (The US Association for Computer Machinery convened a panel on hacking in 1986 which noted that: 'The impetus of being able to perform more and more complex projects can innocently lead the benign user into criminal activity.') Computers generally reduce disparate and remote activities to virtually uniform visual events on the screen. Breaking into a defence research establishment or a hospital data base and erasing information do not appear significantly different from legitimately altering the files in one's own system. Arguments suggesting it would be wrong to criminalise the intellectually curious have therefore repeatedly surfaced in discussions on making hacking illegal. What is certain is that as more and more services are made available on public and private networks the temptations for indulging in hacking will increase.

As a distinctive subculture, hacking first emerged among those who worked in or studied computer programming. Aware of the immense power potentially at their disposal, they found a challenge in mastering design weaknesses in operating systems and extending their knowledge of the geography of computer networks. The more sophisticated manoeuvres and tricks developed by hackers have come from those with considerable programming ability. That knowledge is becoming more and more widely dispersed within society.

The development of hacking has been fostered by the enormous growth in the number of personal computers in homes. Marketed as technological toys with a range of interactive games, they have transformed the worthy work station into playpens for millions of youngsters. Encouraged to buy a modem to connect his machines up to the outside world, the enthusiast learns to roam the electronic highways. Logging on to bulletin boards, he plays the more complex games on offer there, sends messages to friends and picks up a variety of useful tips. The enthusiast may discover how to cut corners and explore lesser-known routes and byways. Eventually he may start hacking his way across international networks, entering unknown systems and opening files of forbidden secrets. To the young enthusiast brought up on electronic versions of games such as Dungeons and Dragons it seems no more than a natural progression.

Edward Austin Singh was always eager to analyse the reasons for his compulsive hacking. He admitted that he was intrigued by the possibility of removing millions of pounds from a bank or spying on military research projects. While still under investigation by the Serious Crimes Squad he confessed: 'Part of it was a sense of power. You were running an informal network of 250 computers and no one else outside your close circle of friends knew about it. The final goal was total world domination, to have everything under your control. It was the ultimate game on the ultimate scale. You got a thrill out of knowing how much power you had. It was possibly hitting back at society. There was a sort of political anarchism involved. The main thrill was beating the system.'

On another occasion he explained: 'It was primarily intellectual enjoyment. I have never done anything malicious, it has always been out of a love of computers. People who release viruses are malicious. I wrote a virus program once but I never used it. Maybe I was being naïve, but there is an informal network of hackers which is highly developed because we trust each other. We traded information with other people about commercial and military systems.'

Later, in a longer statement written in neat handwriting on five pages of a battered notebook, he elaborated on his motivations. 'On many occasions I felt uneasy at getting in so easily. I was worried on behalf of the users. I wanted to help them. To say I was obsessive would be a gross understatement. It often became a fight with fatigue to get a job done. I dreamt hacking – some of my best ideas came from dreams.' The ease with which he broke in generated a growing contempt for the systems managers whom he was outwitting. 'It is hard to remain rational about the state of systems security in the West,' he stated. 'The sheer scope for fraud, espionage and damage has never been greater. What we see and hear about is only the tip of the iceberg. The people who run these systems have absolutely no idea what the hell is going on. It's time they realise that every hacker worth his salt has the likes of a Unix System V internals guide next to him and probably formidable intelligence material at his disposal. The days of kids with just their microcomputers are long gone. This ignorant and stereotyped perception of the hacker is dangerous and foolish. It only serves the purpose of placating corporate, military and government entities.'

Scott Klein graduated to hacking for a similar set of reasons. Taking over a computer by usurping the systems manager's privileges was good fun. 'Would you rather work for a company as an employee,' he asked, 'or would you rather be chairman of the board? Hacking teaches you a lot about computers. It makes you understand more about these machines. And it gives you something to do.'

Another British hacker, who uses the pseudonym 'Shatter', described his initial involvement in hacking as a form of compulsion. 'I would spend twenty-three hours a day at a terminal, and I once managed 103 hours, staying awake with caffeine tablets and cigarettes,' he claimed. 'Sometimes it felt like an obsession. Other times it was just a race against time when you had to get things done before the systems manager came on duty on that machine.' Shatter, in his early twenties, has worked for a British computer security consultancy. 'In America, organisations employ groups of hackers, called "tiger teams", to test out the security of their computer defences. They attempt to break in legitimately. Unfortunately that hardly happens here.'

On bail in West Berlin, Hans Hübner was quite candid about the sense of power he derived through hacking. Sitting amid the 1950s décor of the Wirtschaftswunder Café in the student neighbourhood of Yorckstrasse, he listed the reasons for his involvement: 'Hacking is very addictive and that was the main reason I kept on. It is also a service to others in that it keeps the owners of the networks aware of the problems. They should worry about them. It was great to have systems manager privileges on a machine with sixty or seventy people on it. You could shut the machine down and keep other users out – I didn't do that but it was the thrill of pure power. There you are sitting at home and you can play with a machine on the other side of the world, a machine that might have cost ten or twenty million Deutschmarks. There were times when I was on line every day for ten or fifteen hours. Often it was from 8 pm until 7 am in the morning. To begin with I used my father's telephone and he didn't like me blocking it during the daytime, so I had to hack at night.'

Hübner at that stage – in early 1989 – was suspended from his computer consultancy work in West Berlin while under investigation for allegedly spying for the East. He was convinced his telephone was being tapped. Hübner was not entirely sympathetic towards many of his fellow hackers: 'The general problem of computer people is that they don't understand how the instruments they are using change society. It is important to make them aware of it. They are "*Fachidioten*" – very good at their own profession but not aware of what is going on around them. They are computer freaks.' His concerns illustrate the more political complexion of some hackers in West Germany. 'Cocom is bullshit. At one time we hackers thought we ought to have complete *glasnost* in this area.'

There is a thick vein of rivalry and much heavy boasting out in the networks and on bulletin boards. Reputations among hackers are the subject of jealous put-downs and jeers. The single-minded pursuit of hacking not only confers on the devotee the identity of a rebel, the accumulation of such specific skills also brings for the more talented the possibility of employment as a security consultant. Hacking for some is, in effect, an opportunity of obtaining a privileged computer job and going straight.

In the experience of Detective Inspector John Austen, in charge of the Metropolitan Police's Computer Fraud Squad, hackers can be almost as much a social problem as a criminal nuisance. Intermittently under siege from attention-seeking computer enthusiasts, his understaffed section also has to deal with more serious computer crimes. 'Many hackers seem to want to draw attention to themselves,' he explained. 'I get hackers ringing me up asking me things like is what they are about to do legal. It is a subculture that's growing. One of the ways of becoming a computer security consultant is to break into someone's system and in the resulting publicity offer to show them where the system is wrong. It won't take long for people over here to see that method operating in the United States and imitate it.'

The crossover from curious, if obsessive, browser to determined fraudster is not, so far, a well-trodden path. The vast majority of frauds on the electronic funds transfer (EFT) systems of banks remain inside jobs. Criminal intent is not generally a compelling motive for hacking. There are, however, a number of ways in which computer enthusiasts may be led too easily into conflict with the law.

The largest recurring expense any dedicated home-based hacker faces is the telephone bill. Quarterly bills totalling £1,500 have been waved about by morose youngsters who face having their or their parents' telephones cut off. It is a powerful incentive to take up phreaking telephone lines or using the ID and password of a legitimate account holder on PSS or other networks. A further illicit option is to obtain access to the system of a large organisation, acquire the ID and password of a qualified user, and have all expenses charged to that account. Theft of machine time can be a prosecutable offence.

Vandalism, unfortunately, comes in several computer-compatible forms. Most experienced hackers would consider crashing a system (overloading it so that it switches off, thereby erasing memory sections held in buffers and not stored on disk or tape) to be a sign of incompetence. Intentionally crashing mainframes is something only those in an anti-social or malevolent mood would consciously undertake. At one time, according to Hans Hübner, German hackers considered temporarily knocking out systems a valid sport and signed off with the pseudonym 'Zombie'. Most hackers believe the release of viruses to be an unacceptable activity, although many enjoy the sophistication of virus programs. Viruses and worms, like Frankenstein's monster, are created out of a sense of experimentation. Their subsequent release and proliferation merely serve to advertise the ingenuity of their creator's programming.

Part of the addictive nature of hacking lies in its similarity and proximity to spying. Roaming through the maze of electronic networks, accumulating and piecing together information, trading passwords, deciphering encrypted messages, and operating under false identities, are all skills traditionally associated with the intelligence services. There was even some conscious imitation of this by Edward Singh when, in self-mockery, he occasionally styled himself 'UK Intelligence Officer' in communications with his triad of hackers.

But there are more than just analogies connecting hacking and espionage. Military and defence installations stand out as favoured targets for the more accomplished hacker. Forbidden doors are the most exciting to open, and systems proclaiming their invulnerability are the greatest challenge. Who is not curious about nuclear weapons or space exploration? That NASA has been penetrated again and again is no coincidence.

BEATING THE SYSTEM

Counterintelligence services in the West have therefore had to begin taking an interest in the activities of hackers as well as in the export of computers to the East. At least one hacker has claimed he has an informal understanding with the American FBI to keep them informed of what is going on in the electronic underworld. Others have speculated that intelligence services themselves would be missing many opportunities if they did not occasionally indulge in some network exploration. There is often a reluctance to prosecute hackers who co-operate fully by explaining weaknesses in systems and revealing all their exploits. In West Germany, Hans Gliss, editor of the computer security bulletin *Datenschutz-Berater*, has arranged contacts between groups of hackers and the Verfassungschutz, that country's equivalent of MI5. The victims have also shown a strong interest in the intelligence services' work. There has been increasing demand from commercial organisations for the security and encryption systems pioneered by the NSA (America's National Security Agency) and GCHQ.

Many computer and hacking groups came together not just out of a desire to obtain free calls or subvert systems but because they shared common political aims. In France a group calling itself CLODO (Committee for the Liquidation or Destruction of Computers) claimed responsibility for a wave of attacks on installations in Toulouse. During 1979 and 1980 there were at least ten incidents when activists physically broke into offices, damaged machines and stole tapes and disks. Such Luddite protests were an extreme form of popular fears that the new communication and information technologies were concentrating knowledge, power and profit in too few hands.

John Draper, alias Cap'n Crunch, is one of the folk heroes of the hacking movement, his time in prison in the 1970s for phreaking offences earning him more fame than notoriety. The New Jersey singer, Mike Agranoff, even wrote a poem in his honour, 'The Ballad of Cap'n Crunch', which was published in *2600*, the quarterly American hackers' magazine. 'He would dial up an 800 number,' one stanza related, 'And before the phone rang at all, Give the whistle a blast, dial the number he wanted, And never get charged for the call.'

Draper has been involved in many aspects of hacking and phreaking, most recently as an enthusiastic proselytizer for the San Francisco–Moscow Teleport. He has been keen to promote contacts between Western hackers and computer enthusiasts in the Soviet Union and has established contacts with the International Computer Club in Moscow. As a commercial programmer, he has been exploring the possibility of a new market. As a former phreaker, he also made use of his visit to the Soviet Union. At the Galactic Hackers' Party in Amsterdam in August 1989 – the first international gathering of hackers – Draper gave a lecture on the potential of the Soviet phone system. 'I was there as a citizen diplomat to meet Soviet citizens,' he explained, 'on a special two-week programme drawn up by the Organisation for Planetary Peace.' He pointed out that many Soviet cities do not have direct dialling, and 'Lines are very noisy with static.' On phoning a contact in Lithuania, he remarked: 'When the called party picks up the phone a series of quick pulses are heard. This makes it pretty easy for the KGB to keep track of who phones him.' Having not brought a tone generator along to experiment with, he was forced to the conclusion that the USSR had a wide variety of signalling systems since it was composed of an assortment of German, French and home-made equipment.

Besides Cap'n Crunch, another American hacker who has enjoyed cult-hero status is William Landreth, co-author of *Out of the Inner Circle*, which revealed his electronic exploits. The American edition was subtitled 'A Hacker's Guide to Computer Security, by The Cracker'. The Inner Circle was an informal group of Californian hackers with whom he broke into computer systems. Landreth wrote the book in 1985, when he was twenty, to pay his legal bills. He had been arrested by the

FBI for illegally entering the National Telemail network, which handled electronic mail between NASA, the Defense department and other organisations. *Out of the Inner Circle* was a warning to computer systems managers to be more careful in choosing passwords and avoid using obvious names like Dan, Jim or Lee. Among other favourites, he pointed out, were 'sex' and 'R2D2', the robot in *Star Wars*. Another briefly notorious US hacking group was the '414s', who took their title from the area code for Milwaukee. Among their targets were defence research laboratories in Los Alamos, New Mexico, and several US banks.

Amongst groups realising that more could be achieved by exploiting information networks were telephone phreakers – forerunners of hackers. Richard Neville's *Playpower* published in 1970 as a hippie's handbook and guide to international underground culture contained an appendix on 'Free London'. Alongside sections on Free Travel, Free Funerals, False Addresses and Free Money, one appendix – taken from a booklet called 'Project London' – listed Free Telephoning. Unfortunately, the entry below read: 'This section has been deleted. The original booklet contained detailed information on how to ring anyone anywhere in the world for free.' It was virtually the only subject to be excised from the book which dealt with, among other matters, Dope Data, Growing Your Own, Doing It On The Road, and Fucking The System.

American phreakers were better organised. In May 1971, the Youth International Party Line was founded as an underground newsletter by, among others, Abbie Hoffman. As a leading light in the anti-Vietnam war campaign, Hoffman had already helped create the Yippie Party, an anarchist and hippy alliance. YIPL was a further development of that campaign. In the US, the Government had decided to raise extra revenue for the Vietnam war by taxing telephone bills. YIPL's first issue included a form to send to the telephone company: 'Because of the brutal and aggressive war the United States is conducting against Vietnam,' it stated, 'the amount of federal excise, tax – has been deducted from this bill. Paying the tax means helping to pay for outright atrocities, for the murder of innocent women and children.'

Opposition to the Vietnam war was not its only concern. Its opening editorial declared: 'YIPL will show you why something must be done immediately in regard to the improper control of the communication in this country by none other than the Bell Telephone Company.' Telephone tapping, eavesdropping by the FBI, and how to obtain free calls using the credit card system were also discussed. YIPL was careful to add disclaimers; below an article on blue-box tones its second issue explained: 'Caution – YIPL does not advocate making free calls. However, YIPL does not believe in paying for calls either. If caught you may be charged with fraud and theft of services.' An article by Abbie Hoffman attacked the profits made by AT&T Bell and urged them to reduce the cost of calls, or else 'we'll continue to rip them off'. The open letter ended: 'If you want to discuss this further, call me sometime. Because of all the agencies claiming to have me under surveillance, it's one of the fastest ways to speak directly to your government.'

It was in July 1972 that YIPL carried the headline 'Support Cap'n Crunch': 'The FBI and the phone company have arrested the supposed Cap'n Crunch of blue box fame for allegedly making a few box calls,' it told readers. 'We are now setting up the Cap'n Crunch Defense Fund for the benefit of such obviously political telephone busts. This is needed to show our solidarity against fascist Ma Bell.' The four-page January 1973 issue of YIPL opened with an editorial attacking the military–industrial complex, in which Bell was singled out for special vilification. 'Our purpose is mainly to make people think the question "Why are they ripping off the phone company?" because once they do the answer will be obvious.'

YIPL changed its name in September 1973 to TAP – the Technological American Party. The alteration reflected a change in emphasis: 'TAP is rapidly becoming a people's warehouse of technological information and a name like Youth International Party Line simply didn't ring a bell . . . except of course for the Party Line.' TAP's first issue contained a report of the Second Phone Phreaks' Convention held in a New York hotel. There were fewer FBI agents in attendance than in previous years, the newsletter commented, but 'black masks were handed out at the door for those who felt they didn't want to have pictures taken.' Workshops were held on making blue, red and black boxes, credit card calls, and on 'reforming' the phone company. Among the pseudonyms correspondents to TAP adopted were H. Gordon Liddy (recently of Watergate fame), Almon B. Strowger and H. R. Holdafone. Later issues dealt with a more varied range of technological subjects including burglar alarms, picking locks, altering electric and gas meters and setting up your own radio station. TAP finally ceased publication in 1984 though there have been attempts to resurrect it.

The American hacking magazine *2600* carries on the traditions of YIPL, Draper and TAP, but it covers more hacking than phreaking issues. Launched in 1984, it is published quarterly in New Jersey but can be bought in Britain. A UK newspaper report described it as the 'most direct and single-minded computer anarchist publication'. Among items featured in *2600* have been 'Violating a Vax', how to write worm and password-grabber programs, and 'Getting in the Backdoor – a guide to some popular operating systems'. When Abbie Hoffman died, the magazine's editorial was given over to an appreciation of the hippie guru. 'Abbie was, for all intents and purposes, a hacker of the highest order. No, he didn't go around breaking into computers, although we knew the subject interested him. Abbie hacked authority, which is what a lot of us unwittingly do whenever we play with phones and computers. He stood up to the ultimate computer system known as Society.'

2600 keeps abreast of the latest arrests and busts of hackers, publishes detailed articles on how to hack different operating systems, and surveys bulletin boards and computer networks in

America and abroad. (*2600*, complete with letters from hackers all over the world and a strong editorial line in defence of the right to hack, is available from PO Box 752, Middle Island, New York, USA.)

In Britain there have been fewer organised hacking groups and publications. There is a British version of *2600*, called *2280* – a frequency used by British Telecom. *2280*, however, is published electronically and distributed across bulletin boards. By far the most successful and technically informative is *The Hacker's Handbook* (Century £9.99) which has been through four editions in five years. It was written by Hugo Cornwall, a pseudonym adopted by Peter Sommer, a lawyer and computer enthusiast turned computer insurance consultant; the fourth edition of the *Handbook* was edited by Steve Gold, one of those arrested for hacking into Prince Philip's personal file on Prestel. Sommer's interest stemmed from an early involvement with phone phreaking at Oxford, where he read law.

After university he went into publishing. One of Sommer's authors was the computer scientist Christopher Evans, who later wrote *The Mighty Micro*, a prophetic bestseller about the power of computers. One day in 1968, Evans invited Sommer to act as a guinea pig for his experiments developing user-friendly software at the National Physical Laboratory in Teddington. Sommer was hooked, but he had to wait years before the first home computers in kit form became available. 'The people who knew most about kits were radio enthusiasts and electronics freaks,' he recalled. 'Having a radio licence became very useful. These people were hackers in the first computer sense of the word. My initial unauthorised explorations were through technical curiosity about what people were doing rather than a desire to breach security for its own sake. There was very rudimentary security then; hacking was like going for a country ramble and throwing one leg over a stile. The first bulletin board started in Britain in 1982.'

Sommer expected it to be held within a university mainframe but discovered it was in a personal computer near him in North London. 'You went onto the bulletin board and most of it was quite ordinary stuff. But if the operator liked you or trusted you, he would give you access to hidden hacking sections of the board. The most interesting hacks at that stage were Janet. (The more successful of these explorations were later referred to as "The rape of Janet".) Then one day I found a message on a bulletin board asking why someone didn't write a book about what was going on.' The man who had left the message turned out to be another publisher. Despite initial doubts, Sommer took up the challenge.

When *The Hacker's Handbook* was first published in late 1984 it was condemned by Scotland Yard's Computer Crimes section. Early editions carried details for building a black box, but the publishers removed them from later editions. The later availability of modems in the UK, Sommer once suggested, was a reason for the slower development of British hacking. Sommer's other hobbies have included, he says, 'bunker hunting . . . trying to find out secret sites used by the Government', and a short period spent investigating CB radio when it was first illegal.

In Germany, the Chaos Computer Club of Hamburg, whose hacker conferences Hübner frequently attended, was established in 1981. Its stated aims almost amount to a political manifesto: 'A development into an "information society" requires a new Human Right of worldwide free communication. The Chaos Club . . . claims a border-ignoring freedom of information which deals with the effects of technologies on human society and individuals. It supports the creation of knowledge and information in this respect.' The Club derived its name, according to its official spokesman, Steffen Wernery, from the fact that there is a 'lot of chaos related to the introduction and application of computers'.

Registered in Hamburg as a non-profit-making organisation,

the Club runs its own information service on the German Post Office's Bildschirmtex system. This led the hackers into their first confrontation with the authorities. Wernery and Herwart 'Wau' Holland, the Club's founder, were invited to a conference on data protection and security in Cologne in November 1984. They clashed with Bundespost officials when they claimed there were serious weaknesses in the text system. No one believed them. But a few days later the system had a partial breakdown and the user ID of a Hamburg bank appeared on their screen, together with the necessary password. Using that information, they were able to program a personal computer repeatedly to telephone and then disconnect from one of the chargeable pages the Club operated on the Bildschirmtex system. By the time they stopped the calls the next morning they had run up a bill for DM135,000 (£36,000), which was charged to the bank's ID and account. They informed the Hamburg Data Commissioner about what they had done and told him about the flaw that had permitted it. For several years Bildschirmtex denied that a password and ID could appear on the same systems page. The bank belatedly admitted that the incident had helped improve security.

Early on, the Club issued a code of conduct for its members. They should respect the integrity of any data or files they came across. 'Spoof messages were tolerated,' Steffen Wernery said, 'but no crashing or cracking systems – which is violent or malicious behaviour.' In 1986 the law in West Germany was changed. With a growing awareness of hacking attacks, unauthorised entry into specified secure systems was made illegal. Chaos told its members to desist from hacking where it would break the law. The high profile the Club had taken encouraged it to go down the path of legality. The phrase 'data traveller' was invented by the Club in an attempt to displace the anti-social connotations that 'hacker' held. It did not catch on. Since 1986 many of the more daring feats perpetrated by

German hackers have come from those on the fringes or from outside the Club.

Chaos, as well as lobbying on immediate matters of computer security, also attempted to campaign on the wider implications of rapidly advancing information technology. During the aftermath of the Chernobyl nuclear disaster the Club helped disseminate alternative information on contamination. In 1986 the German Green Party invited the Club to carry out a joint project investigating plans to introduce computer links to the Federal parliament. 'The result that time was a complete disaster,' Wernery recalled two years later. 'In our opinion the politicians had no feeling at all about the consequence of the new technologies they wished to introduce. Problems of privacy, data protection and data security were left unsolved and ignored.'

Chaos holds a convention every year which often attracts computer programmers from other countries. As well as publishing a regular magazine entitled *Die Datenschleuder*, Chaos has produced two large-format reference books. *Die Hackerbibel*, parts One and Two, are anarchic compilations of articles on operating system flaws, reprints of YIPL and other American underground technology magazines, transcripts of conferences, and computer-related cartoons. One American section describes 'The Anatomy of a Hacker' and lists forty known attributes, including: 'Believes the real function of computers is play'; 'Needs no sleep'; and 'Often looks like a dropout from the Woodstock generation'. Elsewhere a reprinted US advertisement promises: 'The Complete Do-It-Yourself Computer Crime System: make big dollars with your computer. Everything you need to use your microcomputer to break into virtually any electronic funds transfer network.'

Hanover's two-week long spring computer fair, which claims to be the largest in the world, has come by tradition to be a gathering point for Germany's hackers. On the last Tuesday afternoon of the fair, members of Chaos and other hacking associations assemble on the exhibition stand of the Bundespost. It is a finely calculated piece of political theatre. Hackers, many of whom spend their time attempting to subvert and obtain free calls from the telephone and data transmission networks operated by the Bundespost, congregate for an irreverent assembly. On the appointed day in March 1989 the Fair's twenty-three exhibition halls had already attracted 392,000 visitors, from businessmen in suits from all over Europe and North America to young computer enthusiasts in jeans and anoraks. The attendance figures looked set to establish a new record as the computer industry pushed the applications of its products into more and more branches of the economy.

On the Bundespost stand, well-groomed staff in blue uniforms, resembling airline stewards and stewardesses, were talking to customers, advising on future communications developments and handing out glossy leaflets. Towards 4 pm the hackers, along with a contingent of curious journalists, began to gather on the stand in Hall 16. The gossip was all about the exploits of two schoolboys who the previous day had, the hackers claimed, been playing around on an exhibit at a stand selling computer software. They had changed the passwords and closed the computer down. Then they had demanded DM10 (about £3) to tell the owners the new passwords they had installed. 'So much for security', the hackers joked, 'if a ten-year-old and a twelve-year-old can hold companies to ransom.' Several hackers handed out stickers with the militant declaration: 'Gib Atari Keine Chance' (Don't give Atari a chance).

Then, from out of the milling crowd, emerged a short man in his thirties with a black beard and wearing a bright-red boiler suit. Wau Holland stepped up to the Bundespost official, Herr Liesche, and presented him with the latest edition of the Club's Hackerbibel. There was applause, a brief speech and the highly groomed hostesses distributed plastic cups of orange and apple juice to the hackers. In the mêlée that followed, television cameras and reporters tried to interview Holland about recently published allegations that German hackers had been spying for the East. 'The best hackers don't go public,' an anonymous youth to one side of the crush explained. 'They would only get arrested. The best people don't belong to the Chaos Club. We are still a country occupied by the US. The Americans tap everyone in Germany through the Bundespost's telecommunications lines. There are rumours that the NSA attended last year's Chaos conference and bugged the lines.'

Later, squatting on the floor near the Bundespost stand, Holland gave an informal press conference on the international aims of the Club. 'There are network links with hackers in East Germany, via Austria,' he explained in his fluent but occasionally idiosyncratic English. 'There are also links with the GDR by radio. It's very difficult there. Few people own modems and the phone lines are very bad. It is just at a beginning stage. Ecological groups are trying to establish links because of pollution in the River Elbe, which is a common German problem. We are in conflict with the authorities because they don't want to give any information about pollution. We try and find out such information for the people, not for the secret services.'

With an air of political enthusiasm reminiscent of the 1960s' combination of direct action and political idealism, Holland expounded his opinions on the way in which societies might be changed by computers: 'It's more interesting to open a society than to open a Vax [a mainframe computer manufactured by Digital]. It will become social hacking. The mass distribution of computers in Eastern countries makes it neat for *glasnost*. It cannot be postponed, the authorities cannot prevent it.' But Holland accepted that there were limits on how open a society should become, and that arguments of data protection and privacy hold some sway. Governments, for example, interfere in private communications by occasionally tapping telephone lines. 'Chaos is between the people who are the victims of new technologies and the politicians and leaders in society who try to manage their information advantages. It would be difficult for us if a group like Greenpeace came and asked us to make a hack. On the one hand we believe this information should be public, but on the other we are within the law.'

Administering the Club is only a hobby. Holland runs a computer systems company which produces software for typesetting and data-encryption programs to help secure communications. 'Our company has an advantage over American firms selling data encryption because they cannot go to the German market because of Cocom. Cocom is totally absurd.'

Although some computer groups hold conferences or meetings, the main forum for daily hacking conversations remains the bulletin boards. As well as being points for exchanging technological know-how, bulletin boards and chat systems function as social centres. One hacker's comment that 'at least one engagement a week is announced between hackers' suggests it is not as male dominated a pastime as is commonly maintained. The names that hit the headlines, however, are usually those of men. Hackers may be seen as a breed apart, but distinctive national idiosyncracies show through. Male Italian hackers, for example, often employ women's names as pseudonyms.

In France, the country's most public videotex system has been employed to further romantic affairs and sex. The telephone company France Telecom encouraged a boom in the use of Minitel – the French equivalent of the UK's Prestel information service – by giving free screens to anyone who wanted them. Minitel is used for anything from home shopping to looking up telephone numbers across the country to finding train times, but it has also become the forum for the less inhibited among the lonely hearts. A user can dial up what has become known as the Minitel Rose service and ask to receive or send electronic billets-doux. Provocative and titillating messages flourished, confirming that the French – even when at a computer screen – have only one thing on their minds. Advertised on billboards and in cinemas, the service was the subject of a book entitled *Minitel Rose*. Minitel may not have been the financial success it was hoped, but its use is more widespread than Prestel. On many occasions, to the annoyance of the authorities, it has also proved to be practical for drug dealers and prostitutes.

In Britain, there are less than 100,000 owners of Prestel Systems, although British Telecom estimates that three times that number are viewers. By contrast with the amorous French, phlegmatic British computer users were a cause of anguish to Ray Thomas, whose sad article was published in *The Guardian* three days before St Valentine's Day, 1988: 'The creativity and tractability of computing gives joy and joy often leads to devotion,' he wrote. 'But devotion can lead to social isolation. Computer systems can communicate but not often in ways which encourage social interactions.' He bemoaned the 'fragmented' electronic mail services in Britain compared to the success of Minitel. 'There could be lonely hearts columns in the computer magazines but they assume the only kind of transactions its readers are interested in are buying, selling or swapping equipment.'

Within the world of private bulletin boards there are specialist hacking magazines produced regularly by groups of friends, some in one continent, some in another. They are often circulated among a number of acquaintances or posted on restricted-access bulletin boards. One such magazine in circulation in late 1988 was *Telecom Computer Security Bulletin*, the product of two hacker groups, Bellcore and Xtension. It opened on a gloomy note: 'Since the demoralization of the underground there has been a rash of information hoarding and a blatant disregard for hacker ethics. This must stop if the underground is to survive. We believe in learning and sharing knowledge.' But it hoped its publication would 'prompt new happenings in the computer underworld. While some of the information contained in these documents may be considered confidential Telco information, we at TCSB are not publishing this bulletin for the purpose of revealing trade secrets or any other implications of industrial espionage, but rather a source of information that we hope you enjoy as much as we enjoy bringing it to you.' Subjects covered in TCSB's first issue included an introduction to the Italian public network, Itapac, written by 'Blade Runner', Digital terminal server basics by 'Mad Hacker', and personal telephone security by 'Byte Man'. The Itapac article includes a section on 'How to Get an NUI'. At a computer exhibition 'Go near the [Itapac] operator and ask: "Is that a modem?". The operator will be moved to pity and feel so relaxed, he types in his password. You, with an optimum eye, must read the keyboard and memorize the NUI. This is called shoulder-surfing.' An article on Primos began: 'This file was to be released in *Phrack*, issue 20, but certain members of that organisation decided that this information was too valuable for release to the general public. You know what I think of that? Utter bullshit. Sounds more like a case of information hoarding to me.' *Phrack* is another hacker magazine widely circulated across bulletin boards, and also specialising in information on networks and operating systems.

Apart from pirated software and stolen passwords, the items on bulletin boards that have aroused most controversy have been those on non-computer topics: stolen credit card numbers, pornography, racist tracts, and terrorist manuals. As an alternative communications network, bulletin boards have highlighted a legal dilemma: are they publications liable to libel proceedings and other restrictions, or merely modes of communication like telephone lines? In 1984 a Los Angeles television engineer operating a bulletin board from home was raided by police who confiscated his personal computer and disks. Amidst the information on the bulletin board were several telephone credit card numbers which had been displayed without their owners' authorisation. The bulletin board operator was charged with wilfully and knowingly publishing the numbers so that people could use them to make free phone calls. He claimed that someone else had put them on his board without telling him and that he was unaware of their presence. Fellow bulletin board operators across the States protested against the case. 'The technology is so new, why do we stop innovation, creativity and free speech so early in the game?' a Chicago lawyer and computer enthusiast asked in the *New York Times*. One way forward, suggested by the paper, was the move towards bulletin boards which grant access only to known acquaintances who are given passwords to the system. Elsewhere in North America the existence of bulletin boards operated by the Ku Klux Klan and disseminating white supremacist literature heightened concern over unregulated electronic publishing. One KKK bulletin board was reported by the Canadian Broadcasting Corporation to have several security levels. Its most restricted area was alleged to have contained the names of those the organisation wished to see dead.

In Britain in the spring of 1989 there were rumours among computer enthusiasts that the anti-hacking bill proposed by the Conservative MP, Emma Nicholson, would include a proposal to license modem users in an attempt to crack down on alleged abuses by bulletin boards. She had been incensed in particular by racist electronic games on bulletin boards, one of which made Jews a target to be killed. Animated erotic sequences were also on display on bulletin boards that could be assessed by young children, she maintained. The suggestion that Nicholson was to propose the licensing of modems was ill informed, but certain boards had already aroused considerable anger among a number of MPs. Writing in the *Morning Star* in June 1989, the Labour MEP Glyn Ford criticised neo-Nazi electronic computer games circulating in West Germany. 'The games, which are illegal and can be circulated easily by computer modem, encourage racism, fascism and outright militarism,' he wrote. 'One such game, called Clean Up Germany, urges its adolescent players to kill vagrants, Greens, homosexuals and Communists . . . Children, the main target for this pornographic material, are told: "All homos have Aids, so fight Aids by killing all homos. Otherwise all normal people in the world will be lost."' Posting pornography on bulletin boards was already illegal under the terms of the 1984 Telecommunications Act, the Home Secretary Douglas Hurd informed a fellow Conservative MP in a parliamentary answer in September 1989.

In April 1988 a long-running bulletin board called 'Corrupt Computing', operated by an eighteen-year-old Coventry student from his parents' home was revealed to contain a section headed: 'Ten Ways to Kill a Cop'. Other files on the bulletin board included details on how to manufacture tear gas, a guide to shoplifting, and advice on what to carry – no address books or identifying material – if taking part in a riot. The student who operated the bulletin board defended inclusion of the items because such information was available elsewhere in newspapers or magazines. Contributions to the board were edited before being made available. His board's telephone number was advertised in a number of survivalist magazines. Nearly a year later a *Sunday Times* story, under the headline 'Bomb Recipes Available on Home Computers', pointed out that a version of the long-controversial text, *The Anarchist Cookbook*, was displayed on a bulletin board in Cheshire. The updated version of the book, the first edition of which was published in Britain in the early 1970s, included 'a step-by-step guide to making plastic explosives, the latest weapon in the terrorist's arsenal'. The board was run by a fourteen-year-old schoolboy whose father maintained that the instructions were inadequate to assemble a real bomb and that much of the information had been inserted by other users of the board. On being informed of the contents of the board, the Tory MP Sir Rhodes Boyson was reported as telling the newspaper: 'This is new and horrifying and there should be an urgent Home Office investigation into what these new modes of communication mean.'

A reminder that hacking, defined simply as unauthorised entry, is not something solely perpetrated by an exclusive class of computer scientists and bored teenagers is contained in the following three stories. Computers have become so user-friendly that playing around on them is a mischievous attraction that even those with no great knowledge of computing can now indulge in.

In early 1989, a senior journalist on the *Wolverhampton Express and Star* was dismissed for penetrating the editor's personal computer files. At the Inland Revenue's offices, underemployed clerical staff were blamed for a string of abusive messages that appeared in computer files containing tax information on individuals. Whenever comments on taxpayers appeared on screen they were signed by 'Hammy the Hamster'. An irate member of the Inland Revenue's Staff Federation remarked: 'Some people see this kind of hacking as a form of light relief.' The third tale was related by Inspector John Austen at a computer conference in London. He recounted the case of a young man who had fallen in love with a policeman's daughter. The suitor gained access to a Birmingham florist's computer and sent the girl a bunch of flowers. On the next day three bunches arrived. By the end of the week there was a houseful of flowers. The policeman investigated and the culprit was caught. Almost anyone can abuse or manipulate computers.

IV

PROFILE OF A YOUNG HACKER

Sredni Vashtar went forth,
His thoughts were red thoughts and his teeth were white,
His enemies called for peace, but he brought them death,
Sredni Vashtar the beautiful.

Saki.

Edward Singh was one of the more talented and notorious hackers forced into the public arena in Britain. News of his arrest by the Serious Crimes Squad was first reported by the magazine *Computing*. Its significance was not appreciated by the rest of the media until details of the investigation were released by the police two weeks later: 'Hacker Cut Into Arms Computers', the *Sunday Telegraph*'s front-page headline declared. 'Singh had developed a program which allowed him access to secrets of the commercial and military world,' the story read. He 'told police he could not only find out details of people's financial accounts but move their money around the world.' The rest of the media presented Singh as Britain's first superhacker.

Singh was then twenty-three years old, an intense young man, intellectually self-assured and consumed by rushes of enthusiasm. When talking he would stare down at the table or

64

floor, his eyes disappearing beneath a fringe of dark hair. He had a talent for missing appointments. He frequently carried around dog-eared copies of philosophical works by Kant, Nietzsche or Wittgenstein in a plastic bag. Dressed in jeans, training shoes and a loose T-shirt, he enjoyed playing fruit machines in pubs, where he would make a pint of lager last several hours. Having left college prematurely, his daily timetable retained the freedom and disorganisation of a student's lifestyle.

Singh's story is in many ways an example of how a fascination with electronics and computers can grow to dominate a young man's life to the point of obsession. He was born on Christmas Day 1964 in Kingston upon Thames, the eldest son of an Indian father and an English mother. When he was three his father died and the following year the family moved to Guildford, where he started school. His interest in machines and how they worked developed early. He first came across a computer at the age of eight on a visit to the Science Museum in South Kensington. 'There was a demonstration of a machine which ran a program called "Guess the Animal",' he recalled. 'I tried to break out of the game program even then. I just wanted to see how the machine functioned.' Later, at the comprehensive school he attended in Guildford, there was an interactive teletype terminal which was connected to Surrey University's mainframe computer. It printed out commands on paper instead of displaying them on an electronic screen. 'There were 1,500 pupils at the school but only two or three of us used the computer regularly. We practised programming in Basic [a standard computer language] and played games. One was a flight simulator called Moon Lander, where we tried to manoeuvre the spacecraft down safely.'

At home Singh's main interest was electrical engineering — with a soldering iron. He would buy old radios and televisions from local scrapyards and try to make them work. Days on end of his holidays were spent in a small workshop in the house's cellar. 'I loved taking them apart. I used to get told off for bringing back all this junk. They didn't understand. It wasn't junk; they were beautiful pieces of equipment.' Having successfully repaired radios, he would scan the dials for unusual stations. Local short-wave band services and Radio Moscow were among his favourites. His ambition at that time was to be a radio officer on merchant navy ships.

When he was fourteen, Singh was adopted and moved to Dorking, although his younger brother and sister both stayed with their mother. The same year he went away to board at a school in the West Country. He did well, passing eight 'O' levels at the first sitting, but he disliked what he felt was an authoritarian regime and asked to be moved. Compulsory church services and an army cadet force were not to his taste. And he did not have regular access to computers.

Back in Surrey, Singh was sent to Brooklands Technical College in Weybridge, where he studied, among other courses, computer science 'A' Level. It was there, at the age of sixteen, he began his first tentative hacking forays. 'I just got hooked,' he admitted. He would spend whole days, often until eight o'clock at night, at the terminal, puzzling out how to explore and subvert programming privileges on the college's Prime minicomputer.

'In some ways it wasn't really hacking because most of it wasn't successful. But one did work: I wrote a capture program that grabbed people's passwords. They thought it was just the terminal asking for their passwords, but it stored them and I would collect them later. I didn't do very much with them when I had obtained them. I just wanted to see if it worked.' His experiments precipitated his first confrontation with authority over the use of computers. 'The lecturers found out about the program and banned everyone from using it. They told me it was illegal and against college regulations.' It did not dissuade him, however, from continuing his explorations. 'Once I got onto a terminal I just got glued to it. People told me I would fail my exams if I didn't do any work. But I didn't.'

BEATING THE SYSTEM

Singh did not enjoy Brooklands and he transferred to another college, this time in Redhill. There he continued his 'A' level course, along with an OND in computer studies and a City and Guilds in computer programming. But he still kept up his hacking. The college's computer was not connected to any external network but it represented a challenge. Singh penetrated it to the point of gaining access to all the passwords used on the system. He was caught again, this time while printing out the complete list of passwords on the main administration department printer. An official spotted the list as it rolled out. Singh failed to turn up for some of his final exams and left with few qualifications.

Out of full-time education, Singh found a job in the mortgage department of a life assurance company, processing application forms and checking credit ratings. A computer terminal in the branch office where he worked linked into the company's central IBM system. It was an obvious temptation. The password necessary to gain access was written on a note stuck to the side of the screen in case any of the staff forgot it. However, the computer was in a busy main office and the opportunity for Singh to use it never arose. He worked there for just under a year but felt frustrated.

In the spring of 1984 he resigned and with a friend set off to travel around North Africa. After only a week of the heat in Tangiers, they decided to return to Europe. 'Even then I took my programmable calculator along with me, a Hewlett Packard HP41C – the type used on the Space Shuttle – and a couple of programming books to keep me company. I couldn't go without them.' Singh and his companion travelled through Spain, France, Italy and down into Greece. By the end of the year they had exhausted their savings. Returning home, Singh had just enough cash left to buy a book on computer operating systems which he found in an Athens bookshop. He read it on the train journey across Europe.

Back home, Singh rented a flat in Dorking with two friends

from college, one of whom owned a BBC microcomputer. From another acquaintance he obtained a modem to connect the computer to public telephone and data networks. Authorisation to use them came with a British Telecom PSS account. His hacking explorations now began in earnest. By dialling up the local university at Guildford, he worked out that he could gain access to distant networks and systems for the price of a local phone call.

Singh was at this time unemployed, surviving on housing benefit and donations from his adoptive parents. 'I was on the computer between six and twelve hours a day. I would wake up and immediately start planning what I was going to do. At home I usually listened to a personal stereo. "The Wall" by Pink Floyd was one of my favourites. Often it was Genesis, Dire Straits or Scritti Politti. When you hacked to music it seemed like it was an art. Caffeine tablets, packets of crisps and cups of coffee would be all I needed to keep going. We didn't have a printer at the flat, so if I wanted a record of what machines I had been into I would instruct the printers at the university to work at a certain time. Then I would go along to the campus and take it off as they printed out.'

Singh's first contact with other hackers via electronic networks came at this time. He was given the number for a bulletin board run by an enthusiast in Leicester. 'That was the first real encounter. Part of the bulletin board was full of hacking information. Through that I got in touch with a guy at Surrey University who taught me how to break into the electronic mail system and read messages. He also gave me a password for a maths department lecturer which was still usable three years after the man had left.'

Early in 1985, then aged twenty, Singh arranged to see a systems analyst at the University's computing centre and expressed an interest in doing work on translation programs between different computer languages. 'I think I was being a bit ambitious, but they were quite keen to help me.' While hacking from home he also enrolled for an 'A' level Computer Science and Statistics course at Guildford Technical College where one of his flatmates was still a student. Singh's reputation preceded him. 'Someone had probably given a reference and warned Guildford I was a hacker. When I first arrived, a notice on the side of a machine in their computer centre said: "Beware – Edward Singh". In the end I was thrown out. I had a letter from the course tutor summoning me to see him. I was told I hadn't attended lectures.'

Most of this time he attempted to penetrate Prime computer installations. Having had early experience of Primos – the operating system used by Prime Computers – he had specialised in hacking into them. 'At that time Surrey University had one of the largest Prime sites in Europe. I managed to get into every computer. We were mainly looking at academic records, administration and telexes.'

Eventually he decided he ought to finish his education. Unlike most aspiring students who select their polytechnic or university on the basis of its academic reputation, social life, or geographical convenience, Singh based his choice on the type of computers on offer. Teesside Polytechnic used Prime computers. It also accepted his qualifications for a four-year BSc course in computer science.

Once in Middlesborough he was quick to take advantage of the computer centre and free programming time. 'By this stage I was getting into commercial systems all over the world. Mostly they were on Prime computers. I had about fifty installations under my belt, machines I could get into whenever I wanted. I hacked with other students there. We were known as the Dot Abuse Kids.' (A '.' – or 'dot' – is simply a common punctuation mark in computer languages.)

As Singh's confidence grew, his range increased. Sometimes his electronic trespassing was noticed. Entering the system at the Edinburgh School of Agriculture for a second time he came across a message which read: 'I know you are a hacker. Ha, ha.' The message asked him to leave the school alone because it was only a small installation and suggested that there were bigger fish in the sea.

It was not long before his activities came to the attention of the Polytechnic authorities. During his first term, Surrey University contacted Teesside and complained that someone was hacking into their computers. Singh was called in. 'They offered me a sort of amnesty, if I gave them a full report of what I had been doing.'

Later in the year, along with a colleague on the course, he broke into a Sussex University computer and found himself talking to a user who said he was the computer systems manager. They did not believe him but the University user insisted they phone a certain number. They dropped the line and called the number. 'The man at the other end said he had traced us back to Teesside Polytechnic and he knew the head of our computer centre. He maintained it was a serious breach of security. In the end I rang them back and apologised for messing around on their systems. Nothing further happened on that occasion.' But he was caught hacking by staff at Teesside several other times. 'Some of the computer staff were afraid in case we should get them all into trouble.'

Dr John Wilford, a senior lecturer on their course, tried to persuade him to stop. 'He was a clever lad,' Dr Wilford remembered, 'but there was something about him that made him a compulsive hacker. Whenever I tried to get him to give it up and attend classes he would become quite penitent and would give it up for a while, but then he would go back to his old ways. It was like he was on drugs. I wanted him to get a qualification and a good job, but he was trying to break into the system code. He did manage to get into Janet, the main academic network, but he was caught by the systems programmers several times. He certainly managed to penetrate quite a few places undergraduates were not supposed to have access to. He was very familiar with Prime, even before he arrived.'

BEATING THE SYSTEM

Wilford believed Singh would have completed the BSc course without problems if he had applied himself. 'I honestly don't understand why he didn't. We tried the friendly approach and we tried the abrasive approach; neither seemed to work. Singh had a very pleasant manner, he was a likable individual, but he hated doing things that didn't interest him. We required some breadth of knowledge from our students. It wasn't for hacking that he had to leave. At that stage he was working in collaboration with another lad at the Polytechnic. He used to spend hours in the laboratory. He would try and break into systems everywhere. We had very little security to protect students from reading other files. He should be employed in some security set-up – otherwise he will end up breaking the Official Secrets Act.'

Singh ignored Wilford's advice, failed to turn up for many lectures, failed the social science course exam and was forced to leave. Hacking, long since an obsession, was now an addiction. 'When I left, I decided I was getting quite far in the context of hacking and it was my only route in computing,' Singh recalled. 'I wasn't unemployable but I would have had difficulty getting a good programming job because no one would give me a reference.'

It was around this time that he adopted a new pseudonym for his expeditions across international networks, that of 'Sredni Vashtar'. Reading a copy of Richard Hillary's *The Last Enemy* – the autobiography of a Spitfire pilot during the Battle of Britain – he admired the name Hillary had chosen for his aircraft. 'Sredni Vashtar' was a ferocious, caged ferret who originally appeared in a short story of that name by Saki. The ferret, worshipped by its young owner, eventually escapes and kills the child's repressive guardian. Singh identified with Sredni Vashtar's avenging power. 'When Surrey University saw the name on their print-outs they probably thought I was a Russian spy.' On other occasions he employed the codename 'Camelot'.

BEATING THE SYSTEM

Returning to Surrey, but this time without a computer, Singh was inspired to find more devious means of obtaining access to computing facilities. 'I went along to the University and masqueraded as a PhD student in computer science. It wasn't very difficult. I could convince the other students without any problem. I knew the campus better than most. I managed to get a student union card during a crowded moment at the freshers' fair.' He had friends on campus and sometimes stayed in university residences. By day, and often long into the night, he would sit at what became his regular terminal. He was accepted as a postgraduate student. 'I was always in the computer centre so people got to know me. Sometimes I would ask for ideas from members of staff, even though I didn't need to know the answer, just to establish my credentials.' The systems analyst who had known him before had left by this stage.

Using passwords obtained several years before, he would log on to the system and then move out from the University into Janet. 'I usually had some objective each time. I would take information along and keep notes as I went. The first thing I would do was make sure the systems manager was not connected up at the same time. I didn't want him watching what I was doing. By the time I was arrested I had mastered 250 systems worldwide. Geographical constraints are irrelevant in the context of hacking.'

Halfway through the academic year the University computer centre realised someone was hijacking their facilities. Surrey's Computer Unit Newsletter for April 1988, posted around many of the 900 terminals at the University, was headed, 'Misuse of Computing Facilities': 'A number of recent incidents have come to light,' it declared, 'in which the Surrey computing facilities have been used for unauthorised activities. The most serious of these have been attempts at hacking.' Hacking, it reminded readers, was the gaining of access to computerised information without authority. It also stated confidently: 'All known incidents have concerned use of terminals to access facilities at other establishments. There is no evidence of any breach of security files held on Surrey disks.'

The newsletter warned that offenders could expect severe disciplinary action if caught. 'Recent penalties imposed at other institutions include an Aston student being fined and suffering a year's suspension, a City user's log-in rights being withdrawn and a Cambridge user having to pay a fine and compensation totalling £500. The specific terminals used in the incidents are known but the culprit cannot be identified with absolute certainty.'

Despite finding a copy of the Computing Unit Newsletter stuck to his regular terminal, Singh was undeterred. The more he hacked, the more hackers he came into contact with, leaving messages or answering queries on bulletin boards and chat systems all over the world. Some bulletin boards were those operated in home computers by enthusiasts who left their machines connected up to the system twenty-four hours a day. Other boards were established in commercial computers, in areas of spare capacity where the company could be unaware of a board's existence. More still sprang up within systems operated by computer manufacturers who wished to attract users and customers to their products and watch them being tested for free. One of the favourite electronic meeting points for hackers in 1988 was the Altos system in West Germany. It was here that Singh met some of his closest hacking colleagues.

In Philadelphia Scott Klein heard about Altos from a bulletin board in the United States. When he was still at school Klein owned a home computer. Eager to obtain more electronic games to play, he bought a modem to connect himself up to other enthusiasts. At that stage his intention was to obtain more commercial software. 'There was one guy who came on to my computer and requested I set up a section for hacking messages, telephone network addresses and system passwords,' Klein remembered years later. 'I did exactly what he asked and before I knew it he had put up the numbers of all the major

US hacking boards. There was one bulletin board in Georgia I tried which had lots of European numbers on it. Some of the European hackers would leave messages on how to get in to Altos. Before I knew it, I was a major force in hacking . . . The chat system in Altos was the best information exchange I have ever seen. If you went in there about 8 pm Eastern US Time you wouldn't believe what was happening. Sometimes you couldn't get on because it was so busy. There would be thirty or forty people in there trading information. Usually there were lots of Italian hackers in there speaking Italian, so you couldn't understand what they were saying.'

Klein, whose hacking pseudonym was 'Szando', also specialised in hacking into Prime computers. 'I thought Prime was a very interesting and flexible type of computer. No computer is difficult if you understand the operating system.' One of Klein's regular hacking companions was a seventeen-year-old from New England whose pseudonym was 'MH'. Klein introduced Singh to MH in late 1987, and for a period of many months they embarked on co-operative hacking ventures, sharing and accumulating information as they penetrated more and more sites.

Singh dubbed them the 'Triad', simply because there were three of them. 'Our methods had nothing to do with Chinese gang warfare,' Singh remarked afterwards. 'Scott and MH used to log on to Surrey occasionally but it didn't hold much interest for them. Usually we would meet up in Altos. It's a marketplace where people trade names and information. Towards the end we used to work together, trading information only with each other.' They held transatlantic telephone conferences to plan their joint hacking operations.

Although often spending four or five hours a day talking, they hardly ever saw each other. There was one exception. In January 1988 MH visited Britain and Singh arranged to see him at Waterloo Station. They spent a few hours in each other's company before MH left for Oxford to attend a course.

Singh and Klein never met. Klein did not know what either of his colleagues looked like. More than a year after his arrest he enquired into Singh's appearance. 'I imagined him having dirty blond hair,' he said, 'being on the tall side, maybe six foot four, wearing glasses and academic looking.' For a police identikit, it would have been more than slightly wide of the mark.

Another hacker whom Singh met in Altos was Hans Hübner. Hacking in West Germany had developed in a more co-operative and politically conscious environment, as exemplified by the Chaos Computer Club. Hübner, then aged nineteen, was on the fringe of the Club, an occasional attender of their annual hacker conferences. He was brought up in West Berlin and as a young teenager had enjoyed constructing electronic kits with soldering irons. He built himself a fuzz box for a guitar, and several radios. 'Then the Sinclair ZX81 computer kit came out,' Hübner recalled, 'a friend bought it and we put it together. At one stage I designed a computer, but I never built it. Gradually I spent less time on the hardware and more on the software. In West Berlin it was only twenty-five pfennigs for a call anywhere in Germany so telephone lines were cheap for hacking. It was addictive.'

Hübner was also involved in politics in Berlin from an early age. 'I was in the house-squatting scene, and the anarchist scene. My parents and family are socialists. My basic attitude is leftist, but I'm more pragmatic – not red or green. Some of those from the Chaos Computer Club were involved in the 1968 era; some are old revolutionaries. Most of the hackers are just computer freaks.' Hübner first ran foul of the authorities early in his hacking career. He was arrested for breaking into computer systems in 1987. 'They busted me for hacking and took away my computer and some of my papers. Eventually they gave them back to me and they never even mentioned hacking when the case came to court. They fined me 500 Deutschmarks for having an unlicensed answering machine connected up to the telephone. That was illegal in Germany.'

BEATING THE SYSTEM

Hübner's hacking pseudonym was 'Pengo' and his West Berlin flat was decorated with penguins. Besides the cutout of a punk penguin singing into a microphone, a tall black papier-mâché penguin stood beside the window, a Penguin Books cardboard cutout in Union Jack colours rested on one shelf, and a painting of penguins hung on another wall. 'When I was fifteen I used to visit the arcades and there was a video game there I loved playing. Pengo was the name of a penguin, the main character in the game. You had to manipulate him remotely to push ice blocks around on the screen.' The name stuck for Hübner's hacking expeditions. He specialised in Digital machines and their VMS operating systems. Like most other hackers he traded information with other enthusiasts. One of them was Singh. 'I swopped some details on line with Edward, but I can't remember what. You never really know where these things are going to go. I never got into a hacking relationship with him.' Singh received several programs from Hübner.

The Altos bulletin board, and later its two-way electronic chat system, had become the main European marketplace for hackers to demonstrate their skills and exchange passwords. For them, it was a secret trading point. For those who monitored the system it was a useful listening post from which to capture intelligence about the electronic underworld.

V

AN INVITATION TO STAY

WITH UNCLE SAM

In the spring of 1988 Singh received a message from a systems programmer at Teesside Polytechnic with whom he had remained in contact. The message, left on the Altos system, warned Singh that Prime Computer's head office in the US was aware of a hacker active in Teesside. A letter from Prime's legal department to the college said the company had isolated a hacker and wanted to be given his name. A new generation of software was being tested at the Polytechnic and Prime was unhappy because its systems appeared to be vulnerable to infiltration. The company feared its work would be disrupted or its programs pirated.

Singh was not surprised to learn they were after him. He had been logging calls out of a Prime machine in the States and had inadvertently recorded his own calls out to other systems. He had left the call logging program on the Prime machine and had only later realised that it might give the company a means of tracing him. After receiving the message from Teesside, Singh telephoned his contact at the Polytechnic and was informed he should get in touch with Prime because they wanted to speak to him. 'I looked up Prime in the telephone book,' Singh recalls, 'and called the then UK managing director, Malcolm Padina.

When I eventually got through, Padina said: "You have been on my machines". We talked about computer security. I criticised the security on his machines. He said if I ever wanted to help him I should write and include proposals.' Thus began a bizarre series of telephone conversations between a businessman turned interrogator and an enthusiastic computer addict suspected of breaking into the company's installations all over the world.

A few weeks later Singh wrote proposing that he should be offered consultancy work with Prime, advising on security matters. Singh suggested a fee of £3,000. He put a hostel address in Leatherhead and his surname on the recorded delivery letter. 'Padina asked me to include some evidence that their machines were insecure. So I photocopied some stuff and sent it off. £3,000 is peanuts for consultancy work. I should have asked for £10,000. After I sent the letter off I didn't hear from Prime for a long time.'

Padina's recollection of the opening moves in their relationship differs in some details. 'I had a phone call from someone called Edward, saying he believed I wanted to talk to him.' At that stage he had no idea who 'Edward' was. Padina had not asked Teesside to arrange for Singh to contact him. 'Eventually he came back and said he was the one who had been doing the hacking. Then I said: "OK, I will talk to you" and we entered a period of conversations. Edward initially offered to sell me evidence of the alleged insecurity of our systems. He wanted to sell documents that would show, so he said, holes in our system. Then, he surmised, we would close them off.' Padina tape-recorded the ensuing conversations.

Padina was surprised to have flushed out the hacker so quickly. He had been informed about the hacking case by Prime's corporate security department in the US. 'They contacted me because they had intercepted traffic and found it was originating in the UK. But they didn't tell me much more than that, just that someone was hacking out of the UK, through Arpanet and into Prime systems in the US. They had intercepted him talking to his buddy. I was told it was something to do with Teesside Polytechnic because they were going to test new software. They wanted the Polytechnic warned about the risks of getting involved in Beta-testing if there was a hacker going in. I wrote to the Polytechnic. The authorities said they were aware there had been hacking going on but believed they could use it to their benefit. And they wanted to continue with the software testing. Within days Edward had got to hear of it and called me.'

After receiving Singh's letter, Prime played a waiting game. Padina took another call in early September from Singh who told him: 'Obviously you don't want to pay me but it's got to the situation where I will help you for free.' So they recommenced their conversations. Padina remembers: 'I would ask Edward why he was doing it. He always said he wanted to work in the computer business. He withdrew his request for money but continued to offer to help and was desperate to help, desperate for the recognition. The thing Edward really wanted to do was to sit down for hours with programmers and discuss the niceties of computer security. At that time I was just a front for the security operation being conducted by the Secret Service and Scotland Yard.'

The operation to trap Singh had been gathering pace for at least six months. Its genesis lay in the United States' Secret Service, the intelligence arm of the Treasury department. The Secret Service is best known for its role in providing body-guards for the President, but as part of the Treasury it also has responsibility for investigating counterfeit currency and some fraud. Under the 1984 Federal computer crime law, the Secret Service was given an enhanced share of responsibility for pursuing alleged computer criminals. The US Attorney General and the Treasury are supposed to have drafted an agreement setting out the respective roles of the Secret Service and the FBI in the field of law enforcement. It did not, however, prevent rivalry breaking out between the two services over which one should be investigating Singh's activities.

The arrest of Scott Klein in February 1988 gave the Secret Service ample opportunity to monitor Singh's network explorations. 'From the beginning the Secret Service knew who Edward was,' Scott recalled, 'but they wanted more information on him. Edward was being set up as well. At that stage they thought he was working with German spies.' Singh did have contact with the Chaos Computer Club and had traded information on American military installations with West German hackers. The suspicion that Singh was a spy was one that gave extra impetus to the Secret Service investigation. In his dealings with agents, Malcolm Padina was given the impression that Singh was at the centre of an international ring of secret agents connected to hackers in Germany. 'What they would have had us believe was that Edward was a key figure in this country,' Padina said. 'They were putting him to me as Mr Big. Edward, they said, was custodian of more information than anybody else, with the capacity to do more damage than anybody else. They thought he was some grand master spy.'

A separate investigation into electronic spying by Eastern bloc intelligence agencies was being conducted by the Americans and the West German Federal authorities. Singh was fortunate that the British police took a more sanguine view of his compulsive hacking. He was also well advised in not accepting what, in effect, was a rather tantalizing Trojan horse.

'After my second approach, Prime offered to fly me over to the States to talk to their experts,' Singh said. It was an attractive offer to an unemployed computer enthusiast who had never been to America. And there was an invitation to work at Prime's research laboratories at their headquarters in Massachusetts. Asked if it had been a conspiracy to send Singh to the States where he could be arrested for hacking offences, Padina said: 'I think it probably was. No one ever said to me, "Malcolm, we want to take him to the States because we want to arrest him". But clearly they would have loved to have had him over there.' And avoid the problem of extradition? 'Yes. I believe the FBI thought he was doing a lot more damage than he was. While talking to Edward about flying him over to debrief him, I could hear the excitement in his voice.'

Detective Superintendent Graham Seaby of Scotland Yard's Serious Crimes Squad, who eventually arrested Singh, later explained the failed extradition attempt: 'The original gameplan was to entice Edward to the US where he could be dealt with by the US Secret Service under US laws. The groundwork was laid. It was tentatively agreed that when Edward put in for his visa it would go through and off he would go. This was one option that was being seriously considered by the Americans in early September. It was accepted at this time that the blackmailing allegation was extremely thin, and there was a realisation that because of the law in this country we would be powerless to do anything. It was quite fortunate in the end that the circumstances of Edward's use of the computer facilities provided a criminal offence, namely burglary. If he had been operating the system from his own terminal over the telephone he would have been virtually untouchable.'

The plan dreamt up by the Secret Service to entice Singh to America was finally abandoned after the US Attorney's department warned it could be construed as entrapment. Scott Klein was also aware of the Secret Service's interest in bringing Singh over to the States: 'It's very difficult extraditing someone,' Klein ventured. 'Dennis Letts told me the second option was to prosecute him under the Official Secrets Act, alleging he had broken into top-secret computers and read classified information.' After being arrested by undercover agents himself, Klein had been threatened with a long prison sentence. He was treated leniently as long as he co-operated.

One of the restrictions Klein was placed under was a ban on using computer systems. He had been charged with breaking into computers and with interstate racketeering and extortion.

BEATING THE SYSTEM

'They charged me because I was trying to get money off computer companies. It wasn't extortion really. The Secret Service was more interested in how I had managed to access the companies' systems. In the Attorney's office they kept on saying to me what I had done was a very serious crime that could be punished by up to 200 years in prison. The judge might put me away for life if I did not co-operate. I was in a state of shock. They come down very hard on hackers in this country. They had put Mitnick away for a year.' Telephone calls to and from Klein's home were recorded by the Secret Service. Engrossed in his hacking activities from Surrey University, Singh accepted Klein's disappearance from the networks and his explanation that his computer had broken down. Their colleague MH was still active.

It was not until a late stage – at the beginning of September – that the British police were brought in. The decision to approach Inspector Austen's Computer Fraud Squad was Prime's. The case was passed on to Scotland Yard's Serious Crimes Squad because it involved liaising with foreign jurisdictions. Seaby, who had recently returned from a research attachment at the Cranfield Institute, where he had carried out his data analysis on computer, was chosen as the man with relevant experience. He quickly immersed himself in the study of computer systems and networks. He held meetings with Prime's American lawyers and learned about the Secret Service's role in the case.

As Singh had used a hostel address in Leatherhead in his letter to Prime, the police could not trace him immediately. In order to arrest him and stop him hacking they needed to catch him at someone else's computer terminal. He was known to have connections with Teesside Polytechnic and was believed to be operating from Surrey University. Detective Inspector Henson was soon able to confirm the name of Edward Austin Singh, but it was not known where he was living since he changed address so often. Surrey University confirmed that Singh was not registered as either a student or lecturer. An electronic trap was therefore sprung on campus to ensnare the elusive hacker.

The University agreed to lay on a slave terminal which would monitor external calls. 'It had to be done skilfully,' Seaby explained. 'We were aware from the trawl of systems we had already done that Edward was capable of scanning systems he used. It was ironic that when he was arrested he had scanned the system, found the slave terminal working, couldn't work out what it was doing and ignored it.' A further problem presented itself. With 900 computer terminals across the campus at Guildford, it was not known *where* Singh would appear. 'We realised that a lot of the material Edward had secreted was on line in various accounts. We arranged with Bill Lennon [the head of Prime's security division] to give Edward legitimate access to an account at Prime's Massachusetts headquarters.'

Singh was put in contact with Lennon by Padina. It was an opportunity for him to demonstrate to the company what he was capable of by sending them some of his stored material. It would keep him on line on a Surrey University computer while he was being traced to a specific terminal, and it would also encourage him to reveal the electronic storage points he was using. 'That weekend it worked. Edward went to the University and did just that. The terminal was identified as being in the main computer block. When I arrived at the University I sat in the security office and watched Edward performing via a video camera.'

That was 9 October 1988. Singh had stayed up until early in the morning at the freshers' disco in the students' union. Waking later that Sunday with a slight hangover, he walked over to the computer centre and at about 3 pm logged on to start a long hacking session. 'I had done quite well,' he remembered. 'I had gone into a few Prime sites abroad. I thought, this evening it's going to be good.' By 7.10 pm he was under arrest.

Singh was connected up to Altos in Germany when Seaby and Henson entered the computer room. Beside his terminal was a piece of paper with many of his account numbers on it. Since he had no right to use campus facilities and the university paper he had printed on was technically stolen, Singh was told he was being arrested for burglary as a holding charge. Singh was wearing a Surrey University Rag T-shirt – a textbook case of 'social engineering'.

Singh's confidence in his knowledge of computer systems and his declared concern for weaknesses in networks had at the same time led him to approach the magazine *Computing*. He had rung the features editor and offered her an article on how computers could be made more secure. The article had not arrived on her desk before he was arrested. The following day the telephone rang in *Computing*'s Soho office. 'I'm sorry I haven't written the security piece,' Singh apologised, 'I was arrested yesterday for hacking.'

Among the pile of computer print-outs the Serious Crimes Squad seized from Singh's grandparents' house in Leatherhead were his notebooks. These recorded the several hundred machines he had gained access to, a variety of passwords, network addresses and user identities. Slotted in between them was a cutting of a column from the *Financial Times* which had been stuck on a sheet of white paper: 'If you are really serious about making a career out of fraud,' the pink cutting read, 'you need to focus on low-profile niches. This means finding large corporate victims who are typically reluctant to admit to being fooled and attract little public sympathy. If fraud is both cross-border and aimed at business victims rather than a wider public, the chances of arrest are virtually zero.' It was not the last time such obvious curiosity would get him into trouble with investigating officials.

Singh's notes reveal a methodical approach. Details of each of the systems he gained access to were recorded in a standard format, listing the name of the installation, the computer type, its operating system, its configuration (memory size and processor model), its network address, and matching IDs and passwords. Beneath each, further comments were added. Under the London Medical Schools, for example, Singh had written: 'March '88. Operating system upgraded. Losing most IDs and passwords.'

The notes also contained several short drafts of articles on computer security. 'Open access allows hackers to gain access to all supposedly confidential information from any non-privileged account,' one section declared. 'It is very rare to come across both internal and external systems whose administrators implement a consistent, rational ACL [access control list] protection scheme. Administrators should ask "Why?" give access and not "Why Not?"'

Singh's conclusions run entirely counter to the commercial notion of computer networks and systems as providing efficient use of shared information. Of his own ability to make use of Prime systems, he boasted: 'Total and complete access to around ninety Primes on Prime Computer Company internal network, ie complete penetration of their network.' He eventually believed he was capable of penetrating any machine on Prime's network. 'With the proliferation of machines on public data networks, the influx of people into computing, and increased communications facilities, the situation of external and internal intrusion can only get far worse. Most external sites have not implemented rudimentary security measures. A radical rethink of systems security is urgently required; however I am not at all confident that this will be the case.'

When Singh was arrested he estimated he had about 250 systems under his control, computer sites he could re-enter at will. 'They were all across the world. Geographical constraints were irrelevant in the context of hacking,' he said. 'I didn't have the resources to handle all the information I was obtaining.' Singh and his colleagues began to satisfy their curiosity by using the world's networks as a sophisticated reference library: 'In 1986 I got interested in particle theory

and broke into the Cern laboratory computers in Lausanne.'
He was able to browse through files on some of the world's
most expensive international research projects. He looked into
the Jodrell Bank's astronomy research centre. Having broken
into NASA he examined details of the Scout Project, controlling
the voyage of an unmanned mission to Mars. He also found
his way into the computer system of a Westinghouse Nuclear
Power Station in the States and explored a space and defence
centre operated by TRW, a US Government arms manufacturer.
In Britain he penetrated into ASWRE (the Admiralty Surface
Weapons Research Establishment).

'I managed to get access to all the files by gaining systems
manager privileges,' Singh said. 'I went into the US Army
systems, but didn't read any of the files. I wanted to see how
efficient their computers were. They weren't so good. I got in
by taking authorisation off another Prime because engineers
were doing work on the Army machines. The UK.MOD. Relay
machine was just forwarding defence mail between this country
and abroad. It might have had some mail from companies
working for the Ministry of Defence. I believe I could have
transferred money around some of the banks I got into. I
broke into Chase Manhattan, Salomon Brothers, Barclays, and
the Security Pacific Bank of America. We got into the money
transfer system of the last one. I was more interested in defence
establishments because they were more difficult to enter. But
I would estimate that seventy-five per cent of computers on
public data networks are insecure.'

Under the heading 'Security Pacific Bank, California', Singh
had written: 'Have access via a PDN [public data network] to
Bank's internal operator programs. Can transfer up to $5 mil-
lion, interaccount. Have around twenty valid accounts, two
with EFT [electronic funds transfer] capability, via Telenet
penetration. SWIFT [Society for Worldwide Interbank Financial
Transactions] access points – further investigating, Telenet
intercepting.' Elsewhere Singh had written: 'Access to SWIFT

node on Telenet. Intelligence indicates message in correct format with bilateral key structure validation will allow fund transfer up to $50 million. Being investigated (via Telenet node intercept).' It was these details that Detective Inspector Henson was most keen to examine immediately after Singh had been arrested. Singh had not moved money around or interfered in the bank's system. He had, however, found the possibility of such action so intriguing that he had discussed the workings of EFT procedures with a casual acquaintance, an employee of a bank in the City of London. The man was later interviewed by the Serious Crimes Squad, who established the matter had never progressed beyond general speculation.

American military installations were a particular fascination. They posed the initial problem of how to get on to Milnet, the US defence network. 'Milnet TAC Dial-up numbers,' an early note is headed. 'Connected on the 703 number, got the following: "Welcome to DDN. For Official Use Only. TAC Log in required." What response do I put to the TAC? Seems to accept two characters before belling. How do I enter authorisation?' Using information on Milnet acquired from the notorious US hacking board P-80, Singh was able to penetrate American defence computers.

Many of the machines Singh found his way into were, in fact, on Milnet, the supposedly secure US military network. Milnet was separated from Arpanet in 1983 because hackers had begun to explore its electronic byways in increasing numbers. 'If people wanted to steal secrets from the military networks they would already have done so,' he said. Other networks were also penetrated. 'At one stage we decided to go in for car design and went into the [–] systems, one in the UK, another in Belgium.' The site on the Continent was sometimes used by hackers to store files. 'Many of these systems were so insecure. At one stage I phoned Oxford University and warned them about penetration, but I don't think any of them took any notice of it. I even sent some electronic mail to Surrey University warning them about hacking.'

'Traded on Shox', Singh had written in his notebooks above a new password to a Vax system. Shox was a bulletin board much frequented by Singh. From it he gained further knowledge of VMS, the operating system for Vax machines. One sheet of his notes records a list of default IDs and passwords that were common to Vax systems unless specifically changed by the user company. 'Even though an account is "disusered",' he wrote, 'such as might be the case with Systest, network access is still available.' He then set out a file transfer protocol method (a means of transferring complete files from one machine to another across a network) that would provide access. In one night, he broke into more than twenty Vax computers on Janet using this method, including Jodrell Bank, the Royal Greenwich Observatory, and the Rutherford Appleton laboratories' astronomy research machine.

Shox was a bulletin board on Altger, the Altos system based in Munich. Run by two Italian hackers, it was closed down in late 1987. Other bulletin boards were later established on Altger. 'Welcome to Shox', the screen flashed up, after the user had logged on. 'Version 2.3. Shell Box for Unix System V by Blueboy, Watson & Marcol. Bulletin Board: List of available files.' On 6 July 1987, the files had included: 'List of NUAs on Janet' by Scooter, 'Advanced VMS Hacking', and 'Itapac [the Italian data network] – Complete NUA List, Privileged!' Among other hackers logged on to Shox that evening, according to the bulletin board's records, were Pengo, Electron, Kilroy, Firefox, Dario, Megabyte, Blackhack, BuckRogers, JohnDoe, Kazuma, Vertigo, Slugbreath, Hacker Smurf, Tekno, Oberon, Maveryk, Lory and Digi. Shox was truly an international trading post. The list of NUAs on Janet had been printed out by Singh. Running to sixty sheets of paper, it contained the addresses of virtually every on-line machine in each department of every university and polytechnic in the UK. Each academic institution was titled UK.AC in contrast to the military notation of UK.MOD. Many of the academic institutions, however, included Government research stations, for example NERC-Oban, NERC-Polaris, NERC Institute of Terrestrial Ecology, as well as the GEC and Marconi research centres, and CERN laboratories in Switzerland.

On one piece of notepaper Singh had listed the British defence installations he had found on the network. These included the UK.MOD.APRE (Army Personnel Research Establishment) and the UK.MOD.ARE-PN (Admiralty Research Establishment, Portsdown). Both worked on Digital Vax machines. Overleaf there was the network address of the US Coastguard in Florida. Numerous machines at the European atomic physics laboratory at Cern were also recorded. On later sheets of paper he had assembled more extensive lists of Ministry of Defence establishments, adding the Royal Signals Research Establishment, and the UK.MOD.RELAY – a military message service. Below this extended list were a number of suggested means for gaining access to the military machines using common VMS system passwords and ways to manipulate the file transfer protocol.

Singh's notebook lists the accounts he had created on the Open University's Digital Vax cluster at Milton Keynes. He had initially obtained access by using standard default passwords and had then created many other IDs and matching passwords. Beside one of them was the comment: 'Taken the system off network pending security tighten up.' Several of his false accounts were then removed. Singh maintains that so many people were using the Open University's resources he telephoned the systems managers to warn them of abuses. In October 1989 the Conservative MP Emma Nicholson said it was estimated that up to twenty per cent of the Open University's phone bill was attributable to hackers.

There were notes on how to phreak several London bank

telephone numbers and on how to obtain free calls worldwide. Of the Strathclyde Industrial Control Unit he wrote: 'May '87 – hacked the Vax 11/750 for some weeks. Then I informed them of the fact. They thought I was an industrial spy! Tried psychological tactics like "You're a lonely person aren't you", while trying to trace my location. Although they never got it. Much fun.' He also copied out several verses of the hacking poem:

> Try to get past logging in,
> Put another password in,
> Bomb it out and try again,
> We're hacking, hacking, hacking.

> Try his first wife's maiden name,
> This is more than just a game,
> But there again, all the same,
> It's hacking, hacking, hacking.

Singh's notebooks, confiscated by the Serious Crimes Squad after his arrest, were returned to him in early 1989. The later computer print-outs from Surrey University – which had been piled up eight inches deep at his grandparents' home – were deemed to be stolen property and were destroyed.

Part of the reason for the successes of Singh and Klein was the programs they developed to intercept calls on the public networks. These were more elaborate versions of mimic or capture programs which fooled callers into believing they were talking to the network's routing system. According to Klein the practice was widespread in the States: 'The public data networks have flaws in them,' he maintained, 'and you can intercept passwords. All sorts of hackers were doing it. We were able to penetrate any system we wanted to by interceptions. The only time you could intercept was before the [network] computer responded to a call. If you hit it exactly at the right time the buffer holding information would be passed to the other person who was calling. You would get passwords and whole log-on sequences. But no computer is difficult to hack if you understand the operating system. You can bypass the security by rerouting the operating system. Other times we would get into the system, get the decryption and decrypt user password files and obtain every user password on the system.'

Singh described their capture programs as 'host emulation' devices. 'We wrote a program that utilised a flaw which allowed us to call into the dial-up node on a public data network,' he explained later. 'The dial-up node has to have an address as well. So we were calling the address itself. We called the dial-up node via the network and did it repeatedly until it connected with an incoming user. The frequency of that coincidence depended upon how busy that particular network node was. It allowed me to connect to the dial-up node at the same time as a legitimate user at random. I would then emulate the system using the false host idea. You mimic the system they are hoping to be in. My program asked the legitimate caller for authorisation and then asked for the network user's address. Once they had connected to my emulation program and entered their password and user name, I would throw them off anyway. If I couldn't mimic their requested system I would pretend to be the system sending back a message saying "network fault". I used to run the program between 1 am and 2 am and would pick up to forty IDs and passwords. It would work for picking up military systems as well as academic and commercial details. No one was exempt! It had to be done at just the right speed otherwise people would have become suspicious. The owners of the networks have known for a long time there were flaws in them. They just didn't do anything about it. Most security managers are middle-aged and come from general security. Their experience is in locking doors.'

Detective Superintendent Seaby accepted that as a hacker,

BEATING THE SYSTEM

Singh was 'technologically proficient, persistent and quite talented'. By nature, Singh, he believed, was a computer addict, not a criminal. 'One of the reasons for Edward's success was his ability to guess what passwords systems used. One of the US Government defence systems he had cracked was using "Ronnie Reagan" as a password. A number of computer companies said they would like to employ him and set him to trying to break into their systems.' In America in particular, hackers are already being used to test the security of their installations, but the problem for many companies, Seaby believed, was that employing someone as well known as Singh might be seen to generate bad publicity. 'At least one thing Edward has done is to bring the matter to the forefront of a number of organisations, both private and government, which up until now had adopted a bit of an ostrich attitude.'

Exactly what confidential information Singh and his colleagues obtained access to must to a certain extent remain unknown. Many of the more confidential systems do not label what they are, and, like most hackers, the subject of Singh's interest was the computer systems, not the contents of files. Whilst at Surrey University he had printed out a long session from an American defence computer to which he had gained access. One of the files contained details of 'Tercom'. It was unintelligible and boring to Singh. His filing cabinet was already overflowing with technical data, so he screwed the paper up and put it into the nearest rubbish bin. Six months later he described having been puzzled by Tercom to a science journalist. She pointed out that Tercom was the name of the computer-controlled guidance system for Cruise nuclear missiles.

Klein was also unsure how far Singh and he had penetrated. 'I'm sure Edward got into confidential computers,' he said, 'but I'm not sure how confidential the information he obtained was. The Secret Service were telling me that Edward got into a geographical service computer that had various pieces of information about oil sites. It had something called a "trophy" on it which warned when you first logged on that it was a confidential computer and that you could be prosecuted for illegal access. Most of the US military computers are not connected to telephone networks and that's for a good reason.' (A 'trophy' is a message that appears on Federal government computers after the user has logged on. It declares that progress beyond that point is not permitted to unauthorised users. The message includes a reference to the relevant Federal act.) Singh admits he saw many such trophy screens and progressed beyond them. Klein, in interviews, maintained he had not been beyond them. British Ministry of Defence computer systems did not post similar electronic warnings to hackers.

Separating fact from fiction was a recurrent problem for the official investigation. One particular piece of paper landed Singh in hot water. It sketched out details of submarine deployment in the Baltic and sites of Soviet SS21 missiles in Eastern Europe. The Secret Service were most worried by it. 'They were quite persistent about it,' Seaby recalled. In fact, the notes were jottings Singh had recorded while watching a television programme on arms control talks. But Singh *had* managed to penetrate the US Defense Nuclear Agency, where he had attempted to run a nuclear war simulation program which included SDI (Star Wars) technology. 'Someone gave me a network address for a computer, so I tried it,' Singh remembers. 'It put me through to another large network and a list of further options flashed up on the screen. I selected a computer called "Bigtop", which was run by the DNA. I managed to guess a password for it . . . the password was also Bigtop. It was a DEC 10 system. I looked around inside. There were lots of files there and I tried to run some of the programs. I had used this type of system elsewhere in England. One of the programs had a lot of simulation material based on wars. We tried making it run, but it kept stopping, as though I was making a mistake. A prompt kept coming up saying "select theatre" and I tried typing in country names but it kept coming back with "select theatre". I just didn't have the expertise on that system to make it run.' The police came across the records of his failed attempt in the pile of his print-outs.

Among computer targets Singh had listed under the heading of 'future projects' were the Inland Revenue, the PNC (Police National Computer), and the Department of Health and Social Security's systems. As Seaby put it: 'Edward had a moral objection to what he termed government by Big Brother and the possibility of linking Government social security computers to the PNC.' Such developments have worried many people, not only Edward Singh.

How far did Singh believe he had penetrated the computer systems he had broken into? 'I penetrated these systems completely. In most cases I could gain super-user or systems manager privileges and get into everything that was connected up to the networks. If I couldn't get in, I would contact someone else via a bulletin board and they would be able to help me.' While browsing through boards in the States he frequently came across ones with valid credit card numbers posted on them. 'It amazed me. There was stuff on there about how to make bombs and manipulate telephones. There are no rules in this game. People don't understand that. Sometimes I would put a back-door into a system and send a message to the systems manager telling him he had been penetrated by hackers and see if he could keep me out. Most of the time they just changed passwords and never found the back-door. You have to be a hacker to catch a hacker.'

One of the favourite tricks of Singh and his colleagues was to intercept electronic messages within companies and send them on. It was through this method that in early 1988 Singh became aware of Prime's internal discussions about hackers. He suspected that they may have been closing in on them. As the company began to track down Singh, he came across a number of psychological profiles of individual hackers. 'They were passing security mail about us which we were reading. Some of it was remarkably inaccurate. The phrase was "emotionally immature". I wouldn't agree with that, but they did describe one of us as "technically proficient".'

Several months after Scotland Yard's investigation, Malcolm Padina reflected on the implications of Singh's exploits. 'Everyone is talking about open computing and access as the way forward,' he explained, 'but having networks you are going to have problems. Is Primos more secure than any other system? A lot of Prime systems are installed. It depends upon the way users secure them.' Padina believed Primos was at least as secure as other comparable leading operating systems. 'Edward Singh was born and bred on Primos. It's easier to get into Prime if you know it. Edward said he found it more difficult to get into another leading operating system but he found it much easier to go travelling around within that system once he was inside it. Other companies are having grave problems to make their systems secure. Primos is as secure as the features you use. Many people do not implement the features provided. It's a question of user discipline. We have been educating our users. Perhaps we even owe a small debt to Edward, that he brought these things to our attention. We have been offering specific training to our users. It wasn't just because of Edward; Prime was becoming a more and more significant supplier to the defence market and Department of Defense rules are strict. [Primos enjoys a respectable C2 security rating in the US Department of Defense *Orange Book*.] I guess Edward made us realise these things are not just a one-off. Security needs constant reappraisal.

'Our corporate security organisation intercepted traffic that eventually turned out to be Edward hacking through Arpanet into Prime systems in the US. When I spoke to him on the telephone I didn't believe he was spying. I don't believe he was doing anything malicious. He was too disorganised, too intellectual. His knowledge was all about the technology. And it was an ego trip. Although we have stopped Edward's efforts, with open systems hacking will become a pastime even more than before. That's why we have to keep going back to our users and keep persuading them to improve our systems. We had hackers before Edward. At one stage, shortly after the introduction of Minitel phones, we had a lot from the south of France. As soon as you are connected to a public data network you are subject to attacks. Hackers will get in through the weakest link. We had a hacker in Scandinavia and he had some connections to our system. From that he could pull files out of our system without ever getting into it. For our own systems we go through a log every day to see who has been trying to get in. We pay special attention to any failures to log on or any calls at abnormal times of the day. So far we have had no problems with viruses. Prime's corporate security department goes around bulletin boards routinely to see what is there.' Electronic smart cards with PIN (Personal Identity Numbers), along with greater use of encryption procedures, were seen by Padina as the best ways of improving security in the future. That Edward Singh chose Prime initially was a matter of chance. Hacking is a problem which every computer company faces.

Several weeks after arresting Singh, Detective Superintendent Seaby arranged for two US Secret Servicemen and a US attorney to meet the hacker they had been shadowing for at least nine months. The confrontation took place, appropriately enough, in a conference room on the campus of Surrey University. Singh believed there was a danger that he might face extradition to America and was also aware the Serious Crimes Squad had not entirely concluded their investigation. He had been warned that inquiries were still being made in connection with the possibility of a prosecution under the Official Secrets Act for breaking into Ministry of Defence computers. With a combined show of modesty and self-assuredness, he said: 'I think it may be a scare tactic. They are making a big fuss out of nothing. I'm not brilliant, but I have shown everything is so insecure. I am just small fry. There are plenty of others who know a lot more than me.'

The interview between Singh and Amaker and Letts did not get off to a good start. 'I didn't really hit it off with the Americans,' Singh admitted. 'They were friendly when they came in. They said "What do you think of Americans?" I said I thought they were a little vulgar. After that things didn't go too well.' There were several computer staff from the University present as well. 'The Americans kept saying "Relax, relax", but there were nine people in that room. The agents knew my life history backwards. They were most interested in talking about military computers. When they went on to talk about Milnet I refused to answer questions. They said I wasn't co-operating and that they had been following me since the end of the previous year. They asked me about the program I wrote exploiting flaws in networks, so I drew it on the board and explained how it worked.'

The meeting lasted seven hours. At one stage Singh put it to Amaker that the Americans were furious with Prime for going to the British authorities. The US Secret Service was not pleased with the suggestion. (In fact the agency never relished their contact with Edward Singh. Ten months after his arrest, a request by the authors of this book for an interview with the Secret Service was turned down with the comment that there was no benefit for them if they took part. 'I think you have the facts of the case,' an agent in the public relations office in New York remarked. 'Since we took on responsibility for hacking in 1984, we have seen a tremendous increase, but it's now beginning to level out.')

As far as the British authorities were concerned, the case against Edward Singh simply petered out. No charges were ever put to him for his hacking. He could not be charged with extraction of electricity because the University had a standard bill for its use of Janet; it did not pay per computer session. There was no evidence of damage to any computer systems and he was merely cautioned for the theft of paper from the computer centre. The facts of his case were also passed, via Special Branch, to the British security services, since there was evidence that he had been inside the ASWRE and other Ministry of Defence computers, although none that he had ever used any of the information on defence establishment files. Publicity about his case added to the pressure for action, and several MPs put down questions in the Commons demanding to know how secure Britain's military computers were. (The Defence Procurement Minister, Archie Hamilton, promised an investigation into the vulnerability of information held on Ministry of Defence systems after one Conservative MP claimed Singh could have 'blown the entire NATO defence system and endangered the world'.) The security services considered Singh's case and the state of the then discredited Official Secrets Act. After the acquittal of Clive Ponting, it was commonly felt that no jury could be relied upon to convict anyone under the old Act, but the new Official Secrets Act did not come into effect until March 1990. In such a situation, the legal case against Edward Singh was allowed to lapse. A hacking martyr was the last thing the authorities were after.

Nevertheless, the investigation was by no means a failure. A number of Singh's British associates, whom he had known through bulletin boards, stopped hacking after reading of his arrest. For Seaby the investigation was a conspicuous success. 'It started out as a blackmail allegation,' he summed up later, 'it went into suggestions of the military security of the Western alliance and of UK Ministry of Defence installations, and ended up as a grand crime-prevention exercise, and possibly even with a change in the law as a spin-off. Edward was brought up short and a hell of a lot of government departments and companies were put on notice.'

Although the American authorities felt cheated, Singh escaped prosecution. His co-hackers in the US underwent long periods of official investigation. The third member of the triad, MH, had his home raided by police in the autumn of 1988 following Singh's arrest in Britain. Neither Klein, who had little option but to co-operate with the authorities, nor MH were held in custody or prosecuted in the end. There was no evidence of them having caused any damage. For a while Singh considered computer consultancy work, but had become interested in medicine as a possible career. MH was at college. Klein was also hoping to continue working with computers professionally. 'I want to become a systems programmer,' he said long after his arrest. 'I'm in the middle of trying to market my own software computer games at the moment.' Had he lost his respect for computer operating systems? 'I think Prime is a very flexible type of computer, very interesting and very easy to learn.'

Over a year after Singh's arrest, the University of Surrey's Computing Unit was still concerned about its involvement. 'Universities are in an impossible position,' a spokesman said. 'We have expensive facilities we try to make available for as many hours a day as possible for students. That leaves us open to people like Edward coming in and using them. Hacking is more often a nuisance than a danger. But we have to take the time countering it when we should be teaching students.'

Singh and his colleagues served to underline a message that was late arriving in Britain. Open computer systems and international networks are not unqualified panaceas opening the way to a brave new information-based society. That message, like graffiti on a high-rise housing estate, is at once alarming and reassuring. Hacking exposes flaws in a planned technological realm. But it also represents an ingenious human recolonisation of a machine-dominated electronic world.

VI

TALL TALES AND CRIMINAL DEEDS

One of the more controversial issues in British politics took on a new dimension in May 1989 when it was claimed that hackers had infiltrated the poll-tax systems of two Scottish councils. The story contained all the appropriate ingredients: a potential threat to civil liberty (in true Big Brother style); the malfunctioning of a computer (to the delight of technophobes); and the threat of a computer virus (to the horror of a society already over-exercised by fear of medical viruses).

The *Scotsman* newspaper reported claims that an expert team of hackers had inserted a virus in poll-tax programs run by Scotland's Lothian Regional Council. Every fifteen minutes for about six weeks, the virus was said to have removed a name from the lists of people due to pay their tax and replaced it with the name of a resident who had recently died. The hackers claimed, according to the story, to have also broken into systems belonging to Tayside Council and the Department of Health and Social Security. The poll-tax protesters refused to reveal their identities but boasted their group contained supporters working all over Scotland, including academics who had 'road-tested' the virus. The anonymous hackers even attracted political support. The *Scotsman* quoted the Labour councillor Keith Simpson, one of those strongly opposed to the imposition of the poll tax, as declaring: 'This is not a virus, it's an antibody. The poll tax is the virus.'

The group's anonymous spokesman claimed to have developed a virulent virus that could reproduce and protect itself so effectively within the system that any attempt to remove it would severely damage the computer program. Lothian Regional Council denied everything. A statement saying it had made 'extensive checks' of the computer system and found 'no trace of this virus or any other unauthorised tampering with the systems', was released to the national press. Instead, the Council blamed delays on the hardware and software, which were 'being addressed as a matter of urgency'. The allegedly indestructible, radical virus was in fact a hoax, but it had forced the Council to step up its security. The phony hackers had made clear their political statement.

The poll-tax episode illustrates the problems of investigating hacking cases. It is difficult, even for the systems manager, to establish whether or not hackers have broken into a data base. No trace may be left if programs are left unaltered, and viruses or Trojan horses are often well disguised. There is a tendency among hackers to exaggerate their capabilities and achievements. Finally there is generally, though less and less, a reluctance to admit that the integrity of computer systems have been compromised.

Hacking, as we have seen, is most often committed out of a sense of fun and adventure. A small proportion of it is perpetrated for political reasons. Very little hacking is carried out for purely criminal gain. Almost all of the recent major computer fraud cases have involved employees. They have been traditional inside jobs made more effective through the exploitation of computers. But many organisations prefer to brand all hacking activities as criminal. For them the recurrent metaphor used to justify this attitude is that of a burglar breaking into a private house.

BEATING THE SYSTEM

Concern began to circulate through the British computer community in 1984, when Steve Gold and Robert Schifreen tapped into HRH the Duke of Edinburgh's Prestel electronic mailbox and found next to nothing. Without the royal connection, their case would have made fewer headlines. But the long-running legal battle through the appeal courts over the legality of their intrusion, and their final acquittal, led to a demand for more evidence of the problems caused by hacking. The anti-hacking lobby, made up of leading computer manufacturers and industrial users, compiled extensive lists of alleged hacking incidents to reinforce their case that hackers should be prosecuted.

Accurate statistics about hacking are almost impossible to obtain from companies and public organisations, who are paranoid about bad publicity. Financial institutions, in particular, have their credibility and customers at stake. Systems manufacturers, who sell their products to the financial community on the basis of a promise to offer high security, are also reluctant to reveal specific cases. In June 1989, *Computer Weekly* exposed the existence of special legal contracts between known computer fraudsters and defrauded companies. Rather than report incidents, some companies were asking the culprits to pay back the stolen funds in return for freedom from prosecution. The Computer Industry Research Unit, a private organisation which collects data on all areas of computing, confirmed that it was aware of at least six cases where companies had attempted to conceal a fraud, including one where £1 million was involved. Many finance houses believe it to be a small price to pay to protect their reputation. To the frustration of the Fraud Squad, publicly quoted British firms are under no legal obligation to reveal that a fraud has taken place. In many American states, financial institutions are required by law to own up to frauds over $50,000.

Yet stories do leak out. In Britain, a hat trick of incidents in 1987 and 1988 threatened to lighten the coffers of three finance houses by a combined total of £42 million. An attempt to transfer £15 million via a personal computer from the London-based office of Mitsubishi Finance International to a City bank over the August bank holiday in 1988 was thwarted in Switzerland. The bank had almost fallen victim to one of the more popular windows of opportunity for financial crimes – the long close-down which permits conventional or electronic frauds to go unnoticed for an extra day. The case was still being investigated in January 1990.

The revelation about Mitsubishi came soon after an attempted swindle worth eighty-two million Swiss francs (£32 million) was made against the Union Bank of Switzerland's London branch. Another, worth £5 million, had been attempted in 1987 against Prudential Bache Securities. In the latter case, two men, Angelo Lamberti and John Filinski, were found guilty of defrauding Pru-Bache after Lamberti tapped out passwords into the company's system from a computer at Filinski's home. Lamberti worked for Pru-Bache Securities in London and through his friend Filinski, a roofer, he was introduced to others who encouraged him to transfer bonds worth £5 million from Pru-Bache to a bank in Switzerland. They had intended selling the bonds through a businessman who believed the transaction was legitimate. In fact, a Pru-Bache employee spotted the suspicious transfer and the bonds were frozen.

In all three cases the culprits were caught red-handed and the victims lost nothing. More recently, in 1989, a financial institution in the City was reported to have had £50 million stolen. The money was divided into smaller packages and dispersed around the world by computer. It was eventually all recovered.

A much earlier case, that of Stanley Rifkin, served for a long time as a paradigm of the huge potential in robbing banks without violence by using electronic deception. In 1978, Rifkin, a computer consultant to the Security Pacific National

Bank in California, sent a fake authorisation, apparently from a legitimate employee, for the transfer of $10 million to an account in Switzerland. The money was eventually converted into diamonds for Rifkin, but he was caught soon afterwards.

Another early American case involving computer deception was carried out by a gang who worked at the Florida race-courses in the mid-1970s. By changing bets placed in the computer system after the races had been run they were able to cream off several million dollars before being arrested. A more recent American case involved the transfer of $69 million from a stockbroker's account at the First National Bank of Chicago to a bank account in Austria in May 1988. Remaining in America, the swindler bought a new house and a Jaguar. But the funds were traced to the US bank account and returned. He is now languishing in prison, serving a ten-year jail sentence.

In the majority of cases of financial fraud, whether paper or electronic, an insider is involved. Often the computer just speeds up or simplifies the old-style crime. There was, for example, the case of the attempted fraud on Britoil of £23.3 million in the summer of 1989. The alleged fraudster's only mistake was to request that the counterfeit paper order be speeded up, thereby alerting a colleague. If the fraudster had merely pressed a few buttons, the crime might have been committed in the blink of an eye without arousing suspicion.

Computers continue to revolutionise the nature of commercial fraud. In 1989, the computer security consultants BIS described the trend of increased use of electronic funds transfer by criminals: 'Often the culprit had to work hard over a number of years in order to build up a private nest egg, even to the extent of never taking long holidays and regularly working late after office hours to force through the illegal transactions or to cover the fraud trail. With electronic funds transfer systems, the fraud only required one high-value transaction to be successfully diverted or initiated to result in substantial gains, and the culprit could afford to retire immediately to South America or the Costa del Crime in Spain.'

With the comparative ease of electronic fraud, the average loss has spiralled from £31,000 in 1983 to £389,000 in 1988. There are more cautious fraudsters who prefer to use the electronic technique of 'salami' fraud. This involves stealing a thin slice – ideally a sum so small as to be almost invisible – from many hundreds or thousands of accounts over a long period. A program is inserted into the computer which instructs the system to remove an amount such as one penny from the target accounts. This is less likely to be immediately detected, but requires patience. The opportunity of getting it all over in one quick transfer must remain an overwhelming temptation.

Age and experience appear to be irrelevant. In 1988 a seventeen-year-old cashier, Timothy Fox, managed to steal nearly £1 million from the Old Brompton Road branch of the National Westminster Bank in London. He had just left school, but soon after joining the bank he learned through gossip at the branch how to move small amounts into his own account without being found out. After two months he had accumulated more than £12,000. In a later, and more daring attempt, he transferred nearly £1 million into the account of a friend, Andrew Kingsmill. Eventually Fox confessed to the initial fraud. During the subsequent investigation he owned up to the more extensive swindle. The two young men, who repaid all but about £15,000 of the total figure, were both sentenced to twelve months' youth custody. The presiding judge at Southwark Crown Court refused to make an order for the remaining money to be returned since it seemed to him that the office chitchat had revealed how easy it was for the fraud to be committed.

The major banks, although the most lucrative of targets, are not the only victims of computer fraud. A favourite playground for some hackers is the networks of the travel trade. In an LBC Radio late-night phone-in in early 1989, hackers claimed a variety of exploits, but at least three admitted to targeting travel agents. In one case, a hacker claimed to have ordered by computer a ticket for a trip to Italy, but on receiving it had – out of fear – torn it up. Claude Misterly, technical executive of the Association of British Travel Agents, admits that the problems have arisen frequently enough for police to take an interest. In late 1989 the police were investigating a young hacker who had ordered a multisector airline ticket by computer, picked it up at the airport and travelled a long way before being caught.

As a result of this incident and many more, ABTA warned its members to tighten up security measures. Only one person, ABTA advised, should know a password to a particular system instead of, as had been the case, two. Agents should check all invoices against reservations and be alert to security breaches at all times. 'Sometimes they are a little careless and do not shield keyboards and screens from the view of the customers. We are asking them to check on that and to keep customers out of staff areas,' Misterly explained.

In a similar case, a flower-ordering computer system was hacked by a youth to impress a girl at his college in Richmond. He ordered three bouquets over the system, but was caught. An associated form of swindle is 'credit carding', when the perpetrator uses stolen credit card numbers. Goods or tickets can be ordered by credit card and sent to a safe address. Hackers of a more criminal bent have obtained valid numbers from credit card companies' computers and, in some cases, from bulletin boards. This is not an easy form of deception since most companies take the precaution of delivering goods only to the address belonging to the original credit card holder. Nevertheless, if a hacker has the criminal intention of stealing credit card numbers, there is the possibility of creating false numbers, names and addresses.

But some of the most impressive hacks have been motivated by the spirit of curiosity rather than by possible financial gain. In the autumn of 1987 a group of peripheral members of the

Chaos Computer Club discovered a loophole in versions 4.4
and 4.5 of Digital's VMS operating system which allowed
them to penetrate 135 networks around the world, including
the Space Physics Analysis Network, which linked research
units worldwide. One of the systems on SPAN was America's
space centre, NASA. The hackers, concerned about security
weaknesses, sought not only the help of Chaos but also that
of Hans Gliss, editor of a leading West German computer
security magazine, the *Datenschutz-Berater*. The hackers felt
threatened after reading messages posted on public bulletin
boards. One widely distributed warning, sent around SPAN
by a systems manager at the European Molecular Biology
Laboratory in Heidelberg, identified two of the hackers by
name. 'Fellow systems managers,' it read. 'Two persons with
known connections to the Chaos Computer Club in Hamburg
. . . have distributed the patches [rogue programs in this case].
They are to be considered amongst the lowest dregs of society.'
The note ended: 'In the hope that someone somewhere will (a)
be saved some hassle from them, and (b) might perform physical
violence on them.'

The story was broken by Gliss in Germany. Chaos, however, was happy to put even more of a political spin on the
affair at a subsequent press conference in Hamburg. The Club
claimed that a large proportion of a 200-page print-out in its
possession proved that much of NASA's research concentrated
on the development of new weapons systems, whereas, Chaos
maintained, it was supposed to be a civilian space research
agency. As the group's spokesman, Wau Holland claimed to
have seen sensitive military information on research into new
weapons systems and rocket accidents. NASA said that the
hackers had not obtained access to any classified information,
only declassified data.

It was this incident more than any other that first publicly
highlighted the enormity of security liabilities as a by-product of
the growth in international computer links. It was embarrassing

not only for NASA but for Digital, whose systems are integral to SPAN, whose links include the US Space Research Center in Los Alamos, California; the European Space Agency; the European Nuclear Research Centre (Cern) in Geneva; and the Japanese space agency. Chaos believed that it was its duty to come out in the open to warn of the possible dangers to which these systems were exposed. Digital, anxious after its operating system had been exploited in the hack, reacted by sending out to all users of the system a free patch (software instructions) which managed to plug the hole in the software. Later versions of the operating system incorporated higher levels of security.

A more curious political protest emerged in Belgium on 22 October 1988. An official investigation had to be launched to discover who had broken into a Belgian Government computer system using the initials WM – the password belonging to the Belgian Prime Minister, Wilfried Martens. The hacker had accessed the Prime Minister's confidential events schedule, which was then passed to a national newspaper and printed. Mr Martens appeared on television to inform Belgium that the system had been revised. The culprit was later discovered to be a Belgian lawyer who had helped design the system but wished to reveal that it was underused.

Not all hacks or interference with computers pose a risk to personal security, but there are reports of incidents that have allegedly caused injury and death as well as huge financial losses. In its submission to encourage the Law Commission to outlaw hacking, Digital highlighted a series of malicious hacking incidents compiled in a report by consultants Coopers and Lybrand. The report lists several vicious examples, including one where a hacker altered the alarm thresholds on a computerised hospital intensive care centre in France, thereby causing two deaths. In another case, logic bombs were said to have been planted in the payroll of a sensitive nationalised industry and then activated during an industrial dispute. The incident precipitated a strike and eventually cost the company around £800,000. In a further case, the report claims a computer file listing AIDS blood test results was copied with the intention of later using it for blackmail.

At the time of going to press, a case was due to be tried of a young man who was arrested in July 1988 and accused of hacking into and damaging files held on computer systems in London, Belfast, Nottingham and Bath. It is the potential risks consequent upon altering data that worry many people inside and outside the computer industry. In a letter to *The Guardian* on 10 April 1989, Ivan Dixon, CND press officer for Exeter, and one of the witnesses on computer control at the Hinkley Nuclear Power Station inquiry, expressed fears over a possible computer virus attack on the systems operating a power station. Even without viruses, he explained, one of the fundamental problems is that it is impossible to be sure that software is 100 per cent reliable. It is widely held that however much theoretical analysis and design is carried out on a software program before implementation, the programmer cannot be certain that it has no flaws. Most software systems have bugs (faults) which are often found only through use. Systems, especially those in safety-critical industries, are thoroughly checked and tested before use, but the risk remains that a bug will slip through. Although the CEGB (as it was then) said it would avoid any links with outside computers for on-line fault analysis, Dixon pointed out that 'even with no outside connections, virus programs or logic bombs can still be imported with new versions of the software or with maintenance programs. It is not safe to assume the system is immune from attack.'

If a virus was to attack the computer system of a nuclear power station, the results could be devastating. Computer viruses have not yet created such a disaster but there are enough around to whet the imagination. As programmers and hackers become more sophisticated so too does the design of viruses. April the first, Friday the thirteenth, Valentine's Day, Christmas Day, a leap year, a boss's birthday or even Christmas – all have had computer viruses associated with them. A new industry is devising products to spot viruses or immunise systems from them; those seeking to play up the medical connotations include Viraid, Data Physician, Check-up and Disinfect. Several books have been produced on how to recognise a virus and how to eradicate it, such as Price Waterhouse's *Complete Computer Virus Handbook*, and S&S's *Computer Virus Crisis*.

Viruses spread quickly when an infected disk is removed from one machine and placed in another, but the program is only passed on to a like machine. There are many viruses but most are restricted to one family of machines or another. Since IBM personal computers and compatibles dominate the market they are the most common victims of attack. The interchanging of floppy disks occurs only with personal computers, so viruses are rarely generated within the larger and more expensive mini- or mainframe computer arena.

The first virus to hit the UK was in March 1988. Called the Brain Virus, it affected the controlling boot sectors of diskettes. The authors and disseminators were two brothers from Lahore. They were motivated to develop the virus, which removed small slices of stored data and slowed down program operations, by wanting to get back at Americans who pirated software. They sold tourists cut-price programs, and when the disks were taken home, the virus spread across thousands of machines. Victims in Britain have included banks, universities, software houses and a hospital.

Later that year, in the summer, a second virus began to infect machines in the UK. At Translation Express, a London company specialising in language translations for business, an IBM personal computer was hit by the Italian 'bouncing ball' virus. The bouncing ball, or ping-pong ball display, is believed to have originated from Turin University. The effect of the virus is to create a bouncing ball which ricochets around the screen, making it impossible to concentrate. The virus meanwhile wipes out small sectors of the hard and floppy disks. Josephine Bacon, managing director of Translation Express, accepted that her company was particularly vulnerable to viruses because it takes floppy disks from freelance translators. Eventually Translation Express had to call in the computer expert, Alan Solomon, whose consultancy was one of the first to investigate the virus phenomenon in Britain. It took a whole day for Solomon to rid Bacon's pcs of the virus.

A pirated copy of the computer game 'Leisure-suit Larry in the Land of the Lounge Lizard' caused havoc in several finance houses in the City of London at the end of 1988. This was a computer game with lively graphics, the object of which was to pick up a woman in a bar, take her home and seduce her. However, the disk containing the game also held a virus. When the game was loaded up the virus began to affect the hard disk of certain pcs, causing some users to lose the entire contents of their disks. The original version of the game, produced by the UK firm Activision, did not contain a virus. This particular scare was also slightly embarrassing for its victims: not only did they catch the virus, they also had to admit to playing with pirated, adult software. Some companies, including the subsidiary of the UK's Dowty Group, went so far as to instruct all staff against using the software on their computers.

Even IBM, the world's largest computermaker, fell victim to a virus written by a member of staff. The virus became known as the Christmas Tree virus because it sent a 'Merry Christmas' message through IBM's internal electronic mail network and at the same time replicated itself, swallowing up valuable disk space. Other supposedly light-hearted irritants have included the Stoned Virus, which flashed up the message 'Your computer is now stoned. Legalise cannabis.' It infected personal computers in New Zealand in 1988, but has occurred in Britain. The virus damages hard disks and diskettes. The American 'Cookie' virus demonstrated a similar sense of humour. Infected machines flashed up the words 'Type in COOKIE'. That temporarily got rid of it, but it reappeared at intervals.

Many viruses and worms cause more trouble, however. The most widespread attack so far came in late 1988 when Robert Morris, a twenty-three-year-old American computer science student at Cornell University, succeeded in temporarily disrupting around 6,000 computers on Arpanet, the network which links up most university research units in the US and includes many involved in sensitive projects for the US Department of Defense, including the Strategic Defence Initiative. The systems breached were mostly Digital and Sun Microsystems machines running the Unix operating system. It turned out that Morris's father was Bob Morris, an NSA authority on the security of the Unix operating systems and encryptions. Morris, Sr, who had developed, but not released, a virus earlier in his research career, defended his son's actions by saying he had written it out of boredom with his college work.

Morris' program was a worm. It was not designed to erase data on any of the systems it infected but simply to reproduce itself, spilling across Internet and snarling up systems as it soaked up computer capacity. The worm contained several hundred common passwords which it tried in sequence in order to gain access to one machine after another. The US Department of Defense claimed no damage had been done to files by Morris's worm, although it was thought to have cost millions of dollars in programming time to check and eradicate the infection. As a consequence, the following year Morris, Jr, became the first person to be charged under the Federal Computer Fraud and Abuse Act of 1986.

His trial took place in January 1990. In the witness box, Morris pleaded that it was a mistake, the worm had spread further than he had intended because of a programming error. He admitted he had been conducting an experiment to take advantage of two security loopholes and believed the program would merely flash up messages to users to alert them to the risks. He did not think the worm would reproduce so rapidly and clog up the networks. But the jury did not accept intellectual curiosity as a sufficient excuse and Morris was convicted. Under the 1986 Act he faced a fine of up to $250,000 and five years in prison.

The 1704 virus affected IBM's customer-training centre in La Hulpe, Belgium, in January 1988. The virus, which gets its name from the way it adds 1704 bytes to a file, has the effect of jumbling the screen with random numbers. IBM despatched warning letters to the 100 customers whose disks might have been infected, fearing they could take it back to their own companies. On that occasion they were lucky and no one confessed to having been infected. A closely related virus is called 1701 and is encrypted.

Another virus to hit IBM pcs and their compatibles is the 1813 virus which originated in Israel. It slows down processes and throws up blotches on the screen. 1813 is also primed to wipe out data on disks every Friday the thirteenth. British Rail admitted in March 1989 that it had been infected by 1813 and reacted – in an unusual manner for most firms in such a situation – by coming out in the open and offering other sufferers a virus detection program that it had developed to help with its own problem. During 1989 the April the first and Friday the thirteenth viruses were largely overhyped, and in some cases files were wiped out but later recovered. Most users took the simple precaution of changing the clock on their machines to avoid the danger dates, thereby preventing an attack. But viruses can take users unawares and cause serious damage if backup disks are not made or also become infected. In 1989, the University of St Andrews' Kate Kennedy Club (an exclusive, public school, all-male organisation) lost most of the names and addresses of old members to a computer virus.

One of the greatest virus scares so far concerned Datacrime, a program which originated in Holland. Datacrime erases the section of the hard disk which controls information retrieval. It was discovered in several computers in the Netherlands in early October 1989. Dutch police put out a national warning and made available 35,000 copies of a software antidote that was said to wipe out the virus. The scare spread across the Channel, where the *Daily Star* first caught on to it with a front-page splash beneath the headline 'Britain on the Blink': 'Britain could be blacked out on Friday the thirteenth next week – by a doomsday computer bug', the story warned. The virus, which is triggered by the date in the same way as the 1813 virus, was alleged to cause a 'threat to our defence system; alert for air-traffic control'; and pose a danger to 'kids' computer games'. In the event, British computers escaped infection, but by then the story had gained a momentum of its own. The Royal National Institute for the Blind was hit by a virus on 13 October, but it turned out to be the 1813 strain. It was eradicated by Alan Solomon, who later said it had caused little damage. Nevertheless, Datacrime was seen to mark a new phase in virus evolution. Unlike the black-humoured, practical jokes in the Cookie, Christmas Tree and Italian viruses, Datacrime was described by one computer consultant as 'bloody-minded vandalism' because of its capacity to destroy so much data.

Another sinister development emerged in December 1989 in a bizarre blackmailing attempt. Up to 20,000 computer disks, describing themselves as 'AIDS Information Introductory Diskettes', were sent out to computer users around the world. Those who received them were on the mailing list of the British computer magazine, *PC Business World*. When the disk was inserted into IBM-compatible machines it ran a program which interrogated the user and used the answers to assess his or her risk of exposure to AIDS. But the disk's real purpose was to insert a Trojan horse program into the user's system. In minute writing, on the back of the accompanying software licence agreement, was a blackmail threat demanding payment of $378 for use of the disk and to receive instructions on avoiding activating the virus. The address for the money was a post-box number in Panama. Several computer security consultants ran the diskette on isolated machines and discovered it was capable of wiping out all the information on the hard disk. This Trojan horse program was triggered by both the number of times the computer was switched on and by reading the machine's calendar. In February 1990, a thirty-nine-year-old American scientist who had formerly worked on AIDS virus projects in Africa, was arrested in Ohio in connection with distributing the diskettes. He was detained by the US Justice department after Scotland Yard's Computer Crime Unit obtained a warrant for his extradition from magistrates in London. The man was reported to be undergoing psychiatric tests.

The incidents of virus and hacking attacks have been widespread and varied, sometimes blurring the line between hacker and criminal. Some hackers plant viruses and then offer to clear systems of viruses and protect them against future attack. In 1989 the first computer crime to reach the Spanish courts involved two technicians who were accused of allegedly infecting municipal computers nationally with a virus and then later offering for sale a vaccine to cure it. But in general, those who are less fond of computers in their own right and see them merely as machines to execute tasks may in the end be more likely to abuse them.

VII

WHOSE FAULT IS IT ANYWAY?

When Pan Am flight 103 exploded in the skies above the
Scottish border town of Lockerbie just before Christmas 1988
it represented one of the most horrific consequences imaginable
of a breach in airport security. A terrorist organisation had
managed to smuggle a bomb into the cargo hold of a New
York-bound jumbo. Even before the immediate shock had worn
off, accusations began to be voiced over responsibility for the
incident. Security at Heathrow and Frankfurt airports were
blamed by some. Some suggested it was the airline's fault, whilst
others said the blame should be taken by Britain's Department
of Transport or the American intelligence services.

Whenever a trusted public transport system fails there is a
hunt for both the immediate perpetrator and for those whose
job it is to prevent such disasters occurring. Often the public
pursuit of the latter is more intense. Breaches in computer
security provoke similar reactions. When hackers break in and
steal secrets, or viruses wipe out vital files, the damage can be
extensive. Systems must be closed down and examined in detail
for evidence of Trojan horses or back-doors which may have
been planted. Files have to be checked to see if they have been
corrupted. Audit trails may have to be studied in an attempt to

track down the culprit. Flaws in the software, which allowed the hacker to take advantage of the system in the first place, must also be plugged.

IBM also used an airline analogy to bring home the extent of the threat posed by hackers. 'If maintenance engineers for Concorde discovered that an intruder had removed the cover panel to one of its engines, the aeroplane would be grounded until the engine had been minutely examined and comprehensive checks made to ensure that it had not been tampered with.'

In the example of Concorde, the security measures would clearly be the responsibility of the plane's operators and not the manufacturer. But in the computer world the manufacturer has a slightly different and closer relationship with the marketplace. There are more new models being tested and produced, and there is a continual demand from users for machines that are cheaper and easier to work with. The demand puts pressure on manufacturers to simplify the user interface of the operating system.

Being easier to use, however, often makes computers more vulnerable, and manufacturers have found themselves in a cleft stick: users are demanding ease of use from their products, but combined with high security. The problem is that it is sometimes difficult to have both. The move towards open systems, where companies can buy products from different manufacturers and link them together, thereby enabling users to shop around for the most economical purchase, requires common standards for networking. Common networking standards and greater ease of access allow legitimate users to benefit, but they also speed the progress of viruses. Common standards may also allow hackers access to even more machines, although set against that, a wider user base enables the computer community to learn about and rectify flaws faster, and, hopefully, open standards will encourage more responsible attitudes.

In the meantime, the increased risks to systems have become

apparent at the same time as there has been a gradual move to the common operating system, Unix, which can be used on all sizes of machines. Unix's flexibility is that the code can be adapted to run on different computers, from personal computers, through minis, to mainframes, thereby allowing programs to be 'portable' (transferable from one machine to another with little or no rework). The advantage of Unix is that a user can buy a computer which runs Unix programs, develop applications on it and then at a later stage buy a different Unix computer from another manufacturer and still be able to run the old applications. If you develop your business applications on an IBM mainframe, for example, the software would have to be rewritten to run on a new Unix box.

The world of Unix sounds ideal but there has been an extensive debate about its security. Unix was originally developed by two engineers in AT&T in the early 1970s. Towards the end of the decade, development split into two streams when Berkeley University took the basic AT&T system and developed its own version. Despite the split, Unix is now beginning to take off in the commercial world. But the danger still remains that greater conformity among operating systems could eventually weaken the collective security of the networks. 'Operating systems are inherently insecure,' according to Peter Jenner, a security consultant with PA Consulting. 'If a person with wide knowledge of a specific operating system gets access, then he or she can have complete control of the system. Software is the weakest link.'

Another reason for the weakness is human error. Software is written by people and flaws creep in. 'What starts out as an exciting job can become boring. The problems come when quick minds get bored. All software projects end up falling behind schedule because managers never give programmers enough time. Pressure gets put on the programmer when the project is delayed. He or she begins to feel undervalued and underpaid. It's a time bomb waiting to go off.' In very rare cases those who feel resentful take retaliatory action which may not become apparent until the software is in everyday use. 'All software has an ego,' says Jenner, 'the ego of the programmer who likes to put something of him or herself into it, something which may or may not create trouble later.'

The most vulnerable operating systems of all belong to personal computers. By definition pcs are designed to be used by only one person. They are simple to use and contain very little protection against unauthorised entry. The word processor used to write this book, for example, does not need a password for entry. Anyone can get into any file stored on its disks. The risks are minimal when the pc is a stand-alone. Only when there are several machines scattered around an office does the security of data become an issue. The first concern is usually to keep it from the prying eyes of a colleague. Outright theft can be the biggest headache for pc users. Lightweight machines have become a popular target for office pilferers. London University's King's College, for example, had 100 pcs stolen in 1989. If the thief takes the data disks with him, then the effect can be more disruptive than an attack by a hacker. Many pc users often end up doing nothing more advanced than locking their machines to the desk.

In fact, users emerge as the weakest link in the security chain. 'People are always the problem,' Nigel Seymour-Dale, IBM's large-systems product manager, observes ruefully. IBM sells a product entitled Resource Authorisation and Control Facility (RACF) which controls MVS security. It puts up barriers to unauthorised users and prompts legitimate users to alter passwords every few days but prevents them from using common words or names. The documentation accompanying RACF emphasises the risks of easy-to-use, high-level query languages. 'An installation can no longer have some security simply because few people know how to access the data. Installations must actively pursue and demonstrate security and use security mechanisms to control any form of access to critical data,' Seymour-Dale maintains. Having created a supposed utopia for the business customer in terms of ease of use, manufacturers now find they have a new range of accessories to sell. The recent obsession with security has primed a large market with a new set of demands from customers.

Manufacturers continuously stress that users should be far more vigilant in the administration of their investment and that they, the manufacturers, can do only so much to protect them. Security is becoming a more significant issue among users who are demanding more powerful versions of pcs in place of expensive minicomputers. Security has also become more important to organisations as more valuable applications are used on pcs and they are linked together into local area networks (LANs). Once connected up through telephone lines to the outside world they immediately become vulnerable to the hacker, both inside and out.

A common method of physically protecting a pc from unauthorised use by those within any organisation is a 'dongle' device which is attached to the outside of the computer and acts like an electronic key. For improved monitoring of remote access, call-back devices are gaining in popularity. These devices are programmed with the telephone numbers of authorised users. When a caller tries to log on, the system will drop the line and ring back the caller's number. If it is not authorised, the line will not be connected. Other sophisticated security methods include using smart cards, similar to cashpoint cards, which can be programmed with a legitimate user's identification details. These devices have two things in common. They are expensive and they slow down the log-on procedure. More futuristic methods may include basing security controls on human biometrics. Voice recognition or eye recognition, where a machine scans the pupil and records the pattern of inner-eye blood cells, could be employed to ensure only legitimate individuals are given access to networks or machines.

Although packing more security features into an operating

system can put a brake on its abuse, manufacturers do not want to take it so far that operating systems become too restrictive. The most secure operating system, for example, is Bull's Scomp, but it is cumbersome and can only be used for limited applications. Nevertheless it has the advantages of meeting A1, the top level of security, as laid out in the US Department of Defense's *Orange Book* guidelines, published in 1983. (A younger relative is the *Raspberry Book*, which sets out similar guidelines for networking standards.) The standards outlined in the *Book* are the ones all computer manufacturers strive to meet because military contracts are lucrative. (The UK's Ministry of Defence follows the guidelines too.) The Department of Defense standards also serve to reassure commercial users who need to keep their data secure.

The majority of established computer operating systems, such as those written by IBM, Digital and ICL, have met the C2 level. Many are awaiting, or have recently received, the higher B1 rating level for the more secure versions of their operating systems. If an operating system meets the C2 criteria (Unix has also reached this level) it means that the security is 'advisory' (the operating system must be able to audit events and keep a record of any unauthorised use so that the system manager can 'be advised' of any abuse that has occurred). To achieve B1 standard, an operating system must be able to restrict usage to an arbitrary group of users. Many operating systems can do this already, but because of inevitable bureaucracy have yet to win the official label.

Manufacturers tweak and update their operating systems frequently to offer better performance and security. In an ideal world a better option would be to rewrite the operating system from scratch, applying security at the very core. But the cost would be crippling to any of the established manufacturers that have invested hundreds of programmer years in their products. To unravel Unix would be the biggest challenge of all. Chris Sarfas, product manager for Ultrix, Digital Equipment's version of Unix, explains that there is too much code in Unix to have it revalidated: 'Because of the way Unix has grown up, there has been input from several places: Bell Laboratories, Berkeley University, from manufacturers like Digital and IBM and so on. It would be difficult to meet the highest levels of security.' Dr Jeremy Turff, of the UK's Networking Centre, believes Unix must change its nature to become more secure. 'In essence it becomes a different operating system. Unix was initially written as a single-user operating system and was not designed to have security built in,' he says. However, the Unix-user group, 'X/Open', dismisses such fears and believes high levels of security can be provided on Unix systems. Adrian Turner, of ICL and a security expert with X/Open, concedes that 'Unix has a worse reputation than it deserves.' Security was not an issue when the operating system was first developed. But since then, he maintains, security has become a priority because of the growth of hacking and through demand from government and defence contractors. Unix has always had the ability to be secure but for a time users did not ensure that it was. The next versions of Unix will have the higher Department of Defense B2 security rating, he said. 'The most secure computer system is a personal computer in a concrete bunker, not networked. But it's also pretty useless.'

The implementation of existing controls and the application of common sense are what most manufacturers advocate as anti-hacking measures. The UK computer manufacturer ICL takes its own security very seriously. An internal document sent to *Computing* magazine included advice on such subjects as the careful disposal of typewriter ribbons in case they fall into the wrong hands and can be deciphered. On the product side, ICL claims that its proprietary VME operating system is one of the most secure available. John Klytta, a VME security expert at ICL, puts such claimed properties down to the relative youth of ICL's offering. 'It was the last major operating system to be developed in the mainframe environment,' he maintained, which meant it took security into account from an early stage. VME is sold with a high-security option which meets the B1 qualification. Nevertheless, Klytta admits, no operating system is 100 per cent secure.

Prime, writer of the operating system Primos, which became Singh's hacking playground, points out that Primos meets the C2 standard when a customer buys an add-on security package and pays attention to basic security measures. Following the publicity over Singh's hacking claims after his arrest, Prime was forced to step up an awareness campaign amongst its users. Prime was frustrated particularly by academics, who, it claimed, were generally less careful about security than other users.

The hacking fraternity is in broad agreement with Prime's case. Although Singh claims he found flaws in early versions of Primos, he believes the real threat to security is in idle or incompetent systems managers who fail to safeguard their systems. The US hacking magazine *2600* supported the same view. The magazine, originally set up in 1984 as a phreakers' newsletter, publishes detailed information on common operating systems. In its summer 1989 edition, a hacker named Violence wrote his own guide to Primos. He explained that the best guide is the real Primos documentation, but accepts that it is difficult to get hold of.

Primos is not a popular target for hackers simply because its user base is smaller than the likes of Digital, for example. The average computer science undergraduate is less familiar with Primos. But Violence suggested that it is an enjoyable operating system to get to know. 'Primos is a very user-friendly operating system and, as such, demands respect,' he warned the reader. Violence also credited Primos for containing certain effective security features ('Its front-door security is excellent') and pointed out that its access-control list 'is almost an impossibility to get around'. Easier to unravel are the password directories, he wrote, and listed some of the more common default passwords used in Primos. He then reminded the potential

Primos hacker that: 'Prime users are people and people like to use easy-to-remember passwords'. Nevertheless, he deliberately maintained some vagueness in the guide. 'I have no wish to compromise any of Prime Computer's trade secrets.'

The computer supplier's case is strengthened further when horror stories emerge about the risks users lay themselves open to. In early 1989 the results of an eight-month investigation by the US President's Council into ten major US Government computer centres – including NASA and the Treasury – uncovered serious security problems relating to the way in which users installed the IBM MVS operating system. The report concluded that many departments proved themselves to be open to fraud, data destruction and the possibility of billions of dollars being sent to the wrong people by a knowledgeable perpetrator, all without leaving an audit trail. The team testing the security had broken into the systems of eight of the centres and disabled them by turning a user terminal into a master-operator console, thereby giving them complete control of the target computer system.

As far as the major threat of viruses is concerned, the only way to avoid catching one is to make sure that any software run on the machine is the bona fide product. There is a host of new products available to protect or monitor personal computers against virus infection. Many continue using the medical metaphor. One, for example, is 'Vaccine'. Supplied by Sophos of Oxford, it inspects a system known to be unaffected and checks for subsequent modifications that would otherwise go unobserved by the user. If a pc develops a virus which cannot be dealt with by the user it is usually a matter of going to one of the new breed of virus troubleshooters – otherwise known as computer consultants. Alan Solomon of S&S Enterprises was the most public of these during 1988–89, when the virus scare seemed to suggest a problem of epidemic proportions. Whenever a virus story appeared on television, or in the national or trade press, Solomon was usually in the forefront dispensing advice. In many cases the viruses dependent on a date trigger were temporarily avoided by simply altering the computer's clock.

A more positive note was sounded by IBM in its submission to the Law Commission, when the company suggested that even if a hacker does make an attack, detection and prevention do not present insurmountable problems. The company's submission pointed out that computers can be programmed to 'detect and identify unusual events such as the repeated use of incorrect passwords or abnormal changes in the use of correct passwords'. It added that electronic surveillance techniques can be used to track a hacker before he or she can even break in to the system. 'In IBM's experience it has not been the case that incidents of hacking come to light only when data is found to have been erased or altered or when fraud is detected. In most, events which precede the gaining of unauthorised access alert the computer owner to the incident.'

IBM, however, also expressed serious concern about electronic eavesdropping, which it believes could become increasingly common as companies store larger amounts of confidential information on computer. A failure to address this issue under any anti-hacking law, the company said, 'will leave a glaring loophole which will be exploited with impunity and at great cost to users of computer systems.' IBM's own staff have expressed concern about this issue through its agony column in the UK subsidiary's in-house magazine. Strangely, the immediate response from IBM management was that electronic eavesdropping is still a low risk since there are usually so many computers running within a small area that it would be impossible to unscramble the electronic emissions from individual machines and convert them into anything comprehensible. Duncan Campbell, general counsel and secretary at IBM UK, responded that IBM itself was taking no special measures to counter vdu eavesdropping. 'Although,' he wrote, 'sensitive operations have been advised to cluster terminals together away from windows.'

Nevertheless, fears about electronic eavesdropping have figured in press reports from time to time over the last few years, with security companies carrying out stunts to prove that data can be read directly from a computer inside a building several hundred yards away. The issue has for a long time been a concern for government and military organisations, who have been aware that the electromagnetic waves emitted from computers can be picked up by relatively basic electronic equipment. According to Rupert Soames, Managing Director of GPT Data Systems, who spoke on the subject at the Resolutions security conference in March 1989 in London, it is 'an unfortunate fact that every length of computer cable is a miniature radio set and with the right receiving systems, which are really very simple, it is possible to listen from several hundred yards away to all the key strokes being entered into a terminal and all the data going into and coming from the screen'.

To guard against this, government organisations employ Tempest technology. This involves encasing equipment in protective, but expensive, metal cabinets or wire meshes, and using fibre optic communications links that do not emit electromagnetic waves. As a result of the expense, however, said Soames, most commercial organisations are studiously ignoring it. It is not surprising. Adding Tempest technology to a system could multiply the cost of the investment threefold. It is also difficult to meet an accepted standard. The only one devised at the moment is NATO's classified standard. Users wishing to use it for their systems must apply to the UK Government Communications Headquarters for permission.

Data encryption can be a very effective security measure, one that is much cheaper than installing Tempest protection equipment. It may not halt the eavesdroppers, but it could prevent them from understanding any encrypted information they may pick up. (To some extent, the world's telephone companies help by packing onto microwave and satellite links as many telephone conversations and streams of data as possible, thereby making eavesdropping on communication lines more difficult.) There are many encryption algorithms (sequences of mathematical instructions) which can be used during the design of a computer system, or at a later stage, to scramble files and messages. Possibly the best known of these is the Data Encryption Standard (DES), now commonly accepted as the international encryption standard. It was originally developed by IBM and the US National Security Agency in 1975 and became a mandatory standard for all federal agencies in 1977.

The DES has been beset with controversy as many security experts and hackers believe it is possible to crack it. Popular opinion maintains that this is a deliberate tactic by the NSA because the US Government needs to be able to read other people's data. It has nevertheless become a widely accepted encryption standard amongst banks. According to GPT's Soames, most commercial organisations make use of fixed algorithms which can be cracked quite easily by someone with sufficient computing power. 'It would not take long to crack the algorithms used on most electronic funds transfer and point of sale systems . . . However, for really secure systems, there is no substitute for encryption where the algorithm is regularly changed,' he explained. 'Typically secure applications in Government use algorithms which would take six months continuous processing to break, and these algorithms themselves are changed on anything up to a daily basis.'

Like most manufacturers, Digital Equipment is critical of the user. But it supports the outlawing of hacking as the best disincentive to abuse, rather than espousing a change in computer design. In its submission to the Law Commission in early 1989, Digital stated: 'The experience of the Digital European security group is that almost all cases of unauthorised access have involved a failure on the part of the user to observe basic security techniques provided. But it is not possible nor cost-effective to guard against absolutely every possibility, in particular because even the most sophisticated security system is only as secure as the honesty of those implementing it will allow. That is why a law is necessary.'

In the future, however, computer manufacturers could be less self-assured if a computer user takes them to court under the Consumer Protection Act. A change in the law in April 1988 shifted the burden of proof for alleged negligence in accidents involving consumers onto the shoulders of the manufacturer. It set nerves jangling in the software community because of fears that software, nearly always beset with teething problems, might come under scrutiny in a court case. At the time of going to press no test case had emerged. Even if it did, the case would be fraught with problems of proof – not unlike the problems which face those trying to prosecute hackers in this country.

Professor Andrew Chambers, Dean of the City of London University Business School, underlined the problems of proving abuse. An accountancy and information technology specialist, Chambers appeared as an expert witness at the Gold and Schiffreen hacking test case. Asked how easy it was to detect and trace back a case of financial fraud from an audit trail, he told the court: 'That's like asking me from which part of which pig a particular sausage came from.' Audit trails might help the systems manager locate penetration of a system, but the work can be painstaking.

Life is no longer made easy for the user, but the risks to his or her system mean that extra security work *is* necessary, particularly if the system is linked to the outside world. In a report published in 1989 by Coopers and Lybrand on behalf of the European Commission, it was asserted that 'network security across European organisations is generally inadequate' – so inadequate that the report foresaw such long-term effects as 'a brake on economic development'. Blame for weaknesses was apportioned to users and vendors alike. Only one of the twenty leading European firms surveyed had adequate security controls, said the report. It concluded that information technology manufacturers had a responsibility to provide better security products. The compilers also discovered that few vendors could supply a comprehensive set of security products compatible across the range.

The Coopers and Lybrand report results are sobering. Most hackers claim that they target systems merely to highlight their weaknesses. While national newspaper reporters break through airport security and pose for photographs on the flight decks of empty jumbo jets in order to show up the flaws in supposedly improved systems, can we blame hackers for having a go?

VIII

WEST COAST ESPIONAGE AND A
GALACTIC PARTY

In the summer of 1986, an academic astronomer, Dr Clifford Stoll, commenced an attachment in the computer department of the Lawrence Berkeley Laboratories in California. His interest lay in developing computer models for cosmological events. He began in the computer administration section, studying the capabilities of the University's machines. One of his first tasks was to run through LBL's computer bills, which were broken down by department. In one bill he noticed a shortfall of 75 cents. His persistence in unravelling this unexplained financial discrepancy resulted in the uncovering of one of the more bizarre espionage episodes of the Cold War.

'If it had been $1,000 off, I wouldn't have thought anything of it,' Stoll told the press later. 'It's like if your house collapses, you assume there's been an earthquake. But if you find a tiny termite hole you think "Geez, I'd better investigate." It's the little problems that are the most fascinating.' The monthly account, to which Stoll tracked the 75-cent sum, showed a user who was no longer accredited to the University. Someone, it became apparent over the following months, was using LBL's computers as a gateway into Milnet, the network linking US defence contractors, academic laboratories and military bases. The mysterious hacker, who employed a variety of stolen passwords and false identities, also broke into a number of the University's departmental computers. In choosing to penetrate LBL, the hacker had in fact confused Lawrence Berkeley with its Californian neighbour Lawrence Livermore, the laboratories which carry out research into nuclear weapons for the Pentagon. Both campuses are part of the University of California.

Following the trail of the hacker, who continued to use LBL computer machine time for his foraging, Stoll came across attempts to discover information on the Strategic Defense Initiative, nuclear and chemical weapons, the North American Air Defense Command, the space shuttle, and crisis management plans involving the US President. The hacker, who was as persistent in his expeditions as Stoll was in the pursuit, broke into the US Army's Optimis computer, the atomic laboratory at Los Alamos, and a large number of installations in the US. At one point, LBL's computer department was contacted by the National Computer Security Center (NCSC), which informed them that an LBL user was trying to get into one of their computers. At the Naval Coastal Systems Command in Panama City, Florida, the hacker copied a file of encrypted user passwords back to his own machine. Later, having cracked some of the codes, he returned to the Naval system and used them to search through more files. The Army's Fort Buckner base in Japan was broken into, as well as the Anniston Army depot in Alabama and the Air Force Systems Command in El Segundo, California.

'I watched as he scanned all their SDI references and the usual pile of things,' Stoll told the *New York Times*, 'and then he started printing out information on the space shuttle. The Air Force told me it was not classified information. Basically the hacker was walking down the street twisting the doorknobs of each house. He wouldn't push hard, but then he would go around and do the electronic equivalent of trying the back door and the side windows. If they didn't budge he would go to the next house on the street.' Exploiting an operating system flaw, the hacker had assumed systems manager privileges on the LBL computer and could create new identities for himself. Rather than change all passwords and eradicate hijacked accounts, Stoll convinced the department to keep watching the hacker and called the police and the FBI to alert them to what was going on.

When the FBI heard that Clifford Stoll was chasing a 75-cent discrepancy they showed no interest. 'They said "What have you lost?"' the astronomer related. 'I said "Well, actually all we have lost is 75 cents". So the FBI said "Who cares; it's not important."' Undeterred, he continued observing the phantom hacker. To identify the hacker, Stoll's wife, Martha, had the idea of creating a phoney computer network in LBL's computers. Stoll called it 'SDInet' and filled it with files of invented information on Star Wars projects. He was confident that the hacker would spend hours browsing through lists, copying files and recording details. In that time LBL, with the help of the phone company, would be able to trace the call to its source through intermediary computer sites. In earlier attempts the call had been traced back as far as West Germany.

The plan worked. For two hours, while the hacker was checking every mention of 'SDI', 'nuclear' and other keywords in SDInet, telephone engineers traced the line through a military contractor's computer system in Virginia and back, via a university computer in Bremen, to Hanover in West Germany. With the help of the West German authorities the hacker was identified, but he was not arrested. The German police said they needed to catch him red-handed to be able to prosecute him.

BEATING THE SYSTEM

The 'SDInet' which LBL set up contained one other trick, however. One of the files mentioned an address at the Berkeley Laboratory where further information on Star Wars could be obtained. When, three months later, a letter was sent from within the US inquiring about SDI, it was given to the FBI, who became interested in the case again. In West Germany the hacker was eventually arrested and questioned by police in June 1987. His name was Markus Hess. After that the hacking through LBL ceased.

Although the American authorities insisted the hacker had not gained access to classified information, there was widespread fear that damage might have been done to the US defence program. In May 1988 Stoll published his findings in a paper in the *Communications of the Association of Computer Machinery*. Entitled 'Stalking the Wily Hacker', it recorded that over the period of a year 450 machines on Milnet had been attacked. Around half the computers had been unavailable. Of the remaining 220 attempts: eighty-two per cent had failed because of incorrect passwords and user names; five per cent had been rejected by the computers because they were not programmed to accept calls from LBL; and eight per cent had given some information on the type and status of the system called. However, one per cent had allowed some sort of access to electronic mail or databases; two per cent had permitted the hacker to obtain normal user privileges; and a further two per cent had enabled the hacker to usurp systems manager privileges. In these attempts the hacker had initially used only obvious account names and trivial passwords. In five per cent of cases he had nonetheless been able to get into allegedly secure US military computers. Only five of all the military sites subjected to the hacking attempts had contacted LBL to say they had traced back an attempted break-in.

BEATING THE SYSTEM

Following the publication of Stoll's paper, the *New York Times* noted: 'The episode raises the possibility that the intruder may have been able to assemble classified data by piecing together data that was sensitive but unclassified. The Reagan administration has been concerned that foreign intelligence agents could piece together classified information by assembling a mosaic of computerized data.' At the same time, the West German weekly magazine *Quick* identified the hacker responsible as a computer science student in Hanover.

After Stoll's article was published, he began working on *The Cuckoo's Egg*, a book about his computer gamekeeping. One of those who heard Stoll's story in the summer of 1988 was Hans Hübner, the West Berlin hacker who was among a number of West German hackers who had been involved in breaking into American computers. But their hacking had become more than a game. The group, which kept its activities secret from the Chaos Computer Club, had established links with Russian contacts in East Berlin. 'I was involved in this,' Hübner admitted later. 'At first I thought nothing would happen. It was just what I did when I was a kid. But I went to the authorities in the summer [of 1988]. Through this story of Clifford Stoll, I feared all of it could come up and I would be in trouble.'

Sitting in his flat in West Berlin in March 1989, Hübner, then aged twenty, smoked roll-up cigarettes as he talked openly about his flirtation with espionage. His role in the events was small, but, he admitted, 'I have been in contact with Eastern bloc groups.' He had by then been questioned by West German intelligence, accused of being a spy, and threatened with jail unless he co-operated.

Hübner first crossed over into East Berlin in connection with his hacking in the summer of 1986. 'I was a hacker at that time and I was only interested in hacking and getting access to more sophisticated machines. What we intended to do was to get a more progressive environment for hacking. I thought they would be putting out money for that. I wasn't thinking much about the consequences. I was only seventeen.' The group had members in Hanover and West Berlin. Of the man they met in East Berlin, Hübner said: 'I don't know if he was a KGB man. I just knew his name was Serge, or maybe Sergei. He wanted us to get software products. The basic trade he intended to do was that we would get proprietary software products and he would pay us money for them. That was contrary to my intentions. I wanted to have a better hacking environment and try and get into more machines, somewhere for accessing the network with unlimited phone bills, where we would be safe and protected.'

Hübner had contact with the Russian official in East Berlin only once. 'He didn't have any technical knowledge or details at all. He said if we had sensitive military information there would be custom for that. Mainly he wanted software for Digital VMS systems. I tried to find software but it was impossible. I was connected to the network with a 1,200 bps machine. That's far too slow to get out a software system that consists of megabytes. I wasn't going to go to Digital and buy a copy. That would be crazy. I did give things that were passed to the Russians. These were software not passwords or secrets.' Among their group there was a belief in a form of electronic *glasnost*. 'We wanted everyone, not just the secret services, to have it.'

Hacking was one way the Soviets believed they could bypass the Cocom embargo on high technology and acquire forbidden products from the West. In *Datatheft*, Peter Sommer, author of *The Hacker's Handbook*, records that the Soviet Union has long been active in obtaining high technology from the West. The activity has even become institutionalised: 'The co-ordination of such activity is handled by the Military Industrial Commission – VPK. This sets targets and priorities between internal customers – the military, research and manufacturing organisations – and the various collecting agencies. . . . The most important of the Russian technical intelligence gathering agencies is Department T of the KGB, and it seems fair to assume that it is they who run any aggressive computer hacking activities, though nothing specific has so far ever been acknowledged.'

'We were real computer freaks,' Hübner said. 'The Russian wasn't very interested in what we tried or how we hacked. His customer, he said, was in Moscow.' Another member of the group was a Hanover student called Karl Koch. 'Koch always pretended there had been deliveries of complete lists of passwords in the US.' Hübner, who was not involved in such activities, remained dubious. Koch was known as a drug addict. 'He had had therapy and took too much LSD and hash,' Hübner commented. 'He believed in all this conspiracy stuff. He thinks he's the hacker who's going to save the world.'

Hübner had not been the first to make contact with the Russian. That was done by others who were not computer enthusiasts. Hübner merely went along with them to East Berlin on one of their trips. 'Many people thought I was the only person in the group in Berlin and therefore decided I was organising it all. I don't know if I was the only hacker who went to the East.' Although working as a security consultant specialising in Unix machines, Hübner's forte was hacking Digital VMS operating systems. He exploited flaws in earlier versions of VMS — corrected by Digital after the NASA break-in. He tried hacking into networks in the Soviet bloc but never succeeded. 'We only managed to obtain the dialling prefix for Soviet systems, but I did go into a number of Yugoslav machines.' One of the machines they went into in the States was Optimis, Hübner said, an electronic mailing system for army officers. It also had a data base of non-classified military information. Many of his colleagues had been into Thomson-Philips, the French defence contractor. 'I can't recall if I had been into LBL,' he said. On another occasion, Hübner and his friends broke into a computer running a police force project in Ottawa. 'I don't know whether it was in operation or just development, but it was full of data about people's hair colour, the colour of their eyes and so on. We didn't know how to start up the main application program and we didn't have time to check it out before they threw us off the system and disconnected their machine from the network.' Hübner was in contact with the group until early 1988, but had stopped being active in their trade with the East long before.

He first approached an intermediary in July 1988, who recommended he contact the Verfassungschutz, West Germany's counterintelligence service and the equivalent of MI5. 'When I first told the German intelligence service they were idiots, they had no understanding about hacking. But I think the US were very worried about what was happening.' The German authorities, already aware of Stoll's story, eventually took Hübner's claims seriously and investigated. On 2 March 1989, in a series of early morning raids by the Staatschutz, many hackers were rounded up. 'The police busted the whole hackers scene,' Hübner said, 'all the guys who have been lawful hackers. At least twenty people were questioned. The police took a lot of computers away. Some people from Chaos thought I should be hung for being involved with the KGB.'

Following the raids, the West German Chief Public Prosecutor's Office in Karlsruhe announced that a spy ring had been broken up. One report claimed the hackers had been recruited in the spring of 1985 by KGB 'middlemen' at the Hanover Computer Fair. Several stories maintained they had been paid both in drugs and cash. Each computer disk handed over was alleged to have been worth DM5,000 (about £1,500). Pictures of Stoll, with unruly long black hair framing his face, making him look like a college dropout, appeared in many magazines and newspapers. He was credited with having first alerted the authorities to the four-year-long trail of computer break-ins spread across Europe, America and Japan. The hackers' activities were said to have added a 'new dimension to espionage'. Their contact, it was alleged, had been a KGB man at the Soviet Trade Mission on Leipziger Strasse in East Berlin. A West German television programme claimed the damage caused was worse than anything since the unmasking of an East German agent in the office of the former Chancellor, Willy Brandt, in 1974. The Federal Prosecutor's office declined to endorse such a comparison. Professor Ulrich Sieber, an expert on computer crime, pointed out that the Eastern bloc had been obtaining Western technology illegally for years. The first East German attempt to penetrate Western computer networks was recorded in 1964, he remarked.

Within the computer community in West Germany and Britain there was a reluctance to believe that hackers were capable of such technical achievements or such treachery. Several writers initially dismissed it as a hoax. At the Hanover Computer Fair nearly two weeks after the arrest, Wau Holland of the Chaos Computer Club said he did not trust the information about the KGB. In April 1989, Herr Alexander Prechtel, a spokesman for the Federal Prosecutor's Office in Karlsruhe, confirmed that: 'This was a ring of hackers, but espionage was not the main point of the ring. The main point was hacking. It is the first time hackers have given information to a foreign secret service. It is not a serious case of espionage, but it is not uninteresting. Any information they did pass was not very sensitive material.'

At that stage only one of those arrested remained in prison. The fact that many of those initially detained were released so soon was merely a reflection of the fact that espionage was considered a relatively commonplace affair. 'In Germany for being a spy the sentence can be from six months to five years,' Herr Prechtel said. 'A sentence under two years can be served on parole. The hackers had an idea they could make money out of it. So they asked themselves who they could make money from. Someone had the idea of giving it to the Russian secret service and they asked an intermediary to go to East Berlin to see if there was any interest. He contacted a member of the Russian Chamber of Commerce in East Berlin who was a member of the KGB.'

One person who apparently found no difficulty in believing in the perfidious nature of many hackers was the Conservative MP Emma Nicholson, who was campaigning for a specific law on computer misuse. The *Observer* in May that year reported that: 'KGB agents are being tutored by British hackers in the latest techniques of breaking into sensitive computer systems . . . Miss Nicholson has passed to the police the names of several Britons alleged to be helping the Soviet secret police. According to the MP, this is being done through hackers linked to Red Brigade terrorists in West Germany, where a web of computer enthusiasts passing information to Moscow was exposed last year.' No associated British arrests have since followed.

The German police investigations continued. Karl Koch, Hans Hübner and Markus Hess had all visited the Hanover Computer Fair in March 1989. None were held in custody. Koch, like Hübner, had approached the authorities before his arrest and had admitted to his activities. Then, at the end of May, he went missing. His badly burnt remains were discovered in woods near Wolfsburg at the beginning of June. The police believed Koch, then aged twenty-four, had poured petrol over his body and set himself alight. Information he had provided, it was reported, had led to the arrests of himself and other hackers in March. Koch's death did not surprise those of his friends who had known of his personal circumstances. Nonetheless it served as a bleak reminder that hacking had become more than child's play.

Contact with the KGB was the subject of an intriguing public debate on hacker ethics between Hans Hübner and Wau

BEATING THE SYSTEM

Holland that August in a converted church in Amsterdam. The confrontation was one of the highlights of The Galactic Hacker Party which attracted several hundred hackers and alternative computer enthusiasts from all over the world. John Draper, leading members of the Chaos Computer Club, American programmers, French Minitel devotees, the editorial board of the New York magazine *2600*, and several Dutch hacking groups were present. Few British hackers attended the three-day party. It was billed as the International Conference on the Alternative Use of Technology and featured network links with Moscow (via the San Francisco–Moscow Teleport), Wellington (where an Antipodean Galactic Hacker Party was said to be taking place), Nairobi, Hamburg and Paris. While the main, though often anarchic, business of the conference was conducted in the theatre, rows of computers were set out in rooms upstairs where hackers from Europe and America swapped passwords and learned new techniques. At one point panic was caused when an electronic message purporting to have been sent by the Dutch police warned the hackers that their activities were being monitored.

The debate between Pengo (as Hans Hübner was styled in the conference programme) and Wau Holland went to the heart of the issue of how hacking should develop. Was it merely electronic piracy or did the hacking movement – as assembled in Amsterdam – have specific semi-political aims? Wau Holland contended that the issue was freedom of information, but some points of privacy had to be respected. Both participants conducted the debate in German. At the same time a translator attempted to keep up with their exchanges and summarise their views in English on a computer screen broadcast to the satellite parties around the world.

Holland opened the debate. 'I am angry and disappointed,' he told Hübner. 'Hackers must trust each other, they must work together. All information should be free. You broke that rule and sold information to others.'

Pengo was unrepentant: 'There is no reason other than fascination for hacking. We contacted them ourselves. I wasn't involved simply for economic profit; it was the technical fascination. I don't see this as a breach of hacker ethics. It was like being in a film you can manipulate. We wanted to be the first and best technical geniuses among hackers. The KGB was real, the contact was real. I can't change the past. I'm working with German agents now.'

Holland grew cross: 'You say there are no absolute rules. I think there are absolute rules in a society. You admit it was like a play? You were a chess piece in others' games. But for them it is the real world. You have destroyed people's trust through your behaviour. Connections with the secret service are serious; you should think first.'

The first hacker rule was that information should be free, Pengo retorted.

'That is an old dilemma,' Holland admitted, 'Who profits? But I have a responsibility. I could kill with the wrong information. We must be responsible. You could hack into a nuclear power plant and cause a catastrophe. Fascination is dangerous. There are limits.'

'The Chaos Computer Club is a group of technofreaks,' Pengo hit back. 'There are no limits.'

Holland would not agree: 'I don't like social control, but individuals must be responsible. The CCC is not a club of technofreaks. We have been interested in the social consequences of computers since the beginning. Our strength is our moral standards. We accept fascination but we are not its slave. Everyone must face the question: "What am I doing?"'

'At the moment I'm trying to do something more positive than working for the KGB,' Pengo explained, at last seeming contrite. 'We are working on an internal network system.'

From the audience a listener enquired whether Chaos was not attempting to impose moral standards that were too high?

'The Germans have such a bad reputation already, one can

not be too careful,' Holland replied. 'We as hackers must face social responsibilities as well. Ideas belong to the world but intellectual property belongs to the individual.'

From New Zealand a remote listener typed in a question: would it be acceptable to break into a multinational company's computer in South Africa and destroy it or give the information to the African National Congress?

The query was left unanswered by the two protagonists. Half a generation apart, the confrontation resembled a culture clash between a hippy and a punk – perhaps a cyberpunk.

Ethics was just one of many topics fought over at the Galactic Hacker Party. There were discussions on the relationship between the human brain and the computer, on the links between ecological groups and alternative computer networks, on how hackers and intelligence services interact, on viruses, censorship in bulletin boards, fascist computer games, and hacking legislation. The conference embraced both senses of the word 'hacker' – the creative computer programmer and the more recent meaning of someone who tries to break into the networks and systems of others. The participants were generally a mixture of West Coast computer veterans and younger European hackers. Few women were present, but there were computer musicians, a Dutch Professor of Andragology (described as the science of social change), the French author of a hacker thriller, political scientists and telecommunications experts – a sufficiently heterodox gathering for the first international hackers' conference. In the programme, the Chaos Computer Club – motto: use public data freely; protect private data firmly – was described as having become a legend in hacking. Due to the prevailing 'German socio-political climate it was increasingly viewed as a radical political movement with consequent harassment from the authorities'. A Dutch hacker magazine, *Hack-Tic*, was another of the Galactic Party organisers.

BEATING THE SYSTEM

The proceedings at the Paradiso opened at 10 am on 2 August 1989. A giant white curtain hung over the stage decorated with the title 'Galactic Hacker Party'. Banks of computers had been set up beneath the stage. A large video screen stood over the computers. No one introduced the session formally. Hackers can be poor communicators. Perplexed journalists and camera crews watched expectantly. The video screen crackled and suddenly came to life. A revoiced version of the mock computer video jockey, Max Headroom – 'Hacking the computers others are afraid to access' – began playing. 'Just run to the first computer you see and hack as much as possible,' his image urged. 'Do you know how much my phone bill is? Only £10. Thank you, AT&T. I think I'm going off line now,' and the screen went blank. Cap'n Crunch, bespectacled, bearded, and with greying curly hair, took over from the video with a display of the Moscow–San Francisco Teleport.

Several US jail sentences had not dimmed John Draper's enthusiasm for technical gadgets. Providing a running commentary through a microphone, Draper explained the operations necessary to establish contact with the Soviet capital. 'Sometimes the network can be congested and rather slow,' he apologised as the projected computer screen registered no response from Moscow or San Francisco. Draper typed in another sequence of commands. Making a direct phone call to Russia might have been quicker. 'Just now the Soviet people are getting into networking. They are not yet used to the idea of electronic mail. Sometimes you have to give these people a kick to get started.' Finally he announced: 'We have ten people from the Soviet Union on line with us now.' Vladimir Perov, aged twenty-four, from the Novosobirsk Technical Institute typed in his question: 'What do you know about object-oriented programming?' (Object-oriented programming was the latest software craze in the States.) The West's finest hackers sent back a different type of question. 'Do the Soviets think of themselves as part of the global village of computer networks?'

a Dutch youth asked. 'Is there use of computers by private citizens and how easy is it to obtain them?' a more suspicious questioner enquired. The Teleport is also capable of taking and transmitting pictures. Amsterdam and Moscow exchanged freeze frames of each other sitting at their terminals. It was not so hot as photography goes, but it was a new gadget for the technologically-minded to exploit.

Another West Coast veteran was Lee Felsenstein, who had cut his first political teeth on the campus protest movements in Berkeley in the 1960s. He delivered the conference's keynote address under the title of 'The Computer as a Tool for Democracy'. 'We have within our grasp the means of implementing a new participatory democracy,' he claimed. 'The aim is to create a tool for the refoundation of communities.' Felsenstein had been nineteen in 1964 when the first of the campus rebellions – the free-speech movement – came to Berkeley. A technology student, he was as enthusiastic as the rest, but felt himself a follower in the movement. 'I hung around the students' headquarters,' he confessed. 'Then one day two students came running into the room and said the police had surrounded the campus. It seemed to me that everyone in that room turned to me and said "Make us a policeman's radio". It was the work of a few minutes. At that moment I realised that although I thought I was a follower, I was in fact a leader. Technologists make choices which define the boundaries of political action.'

For Felsenstein, computer networks stand as a means for integrating society 'horizontally' and destroying the hierarchical structures of society. 'The technology exists through which the myth of the hierarchical organisation structure can be put to rest. This will be done through consciously empowering the Agora Function [the agora being the Greek equivalent of the Roman forum, ie the marketplace for exchanging information] in a telecommunication space. The widespread availability of the Agora Function will create the possibility of a transition to a post-hierarchical or participatory democratic society. We technologists have never shrunk from doing that which is considered impossible. We have the opportunity to accept our position and transform society.' It sounded like high-flown rhetoric anchored by few practical suggestions. But Felsenstein reminded his audience that he and other members of the West Coast-based Homebrew Computer Club in the mid-1970s had dreamt up the idea of personal computers. 'A group of technos got together to learn from and teach each other. We made available one of the first personal computer kits. Four companies are still in existence, having come out of the Homebrew Computer Club – one of them is Apple. We worked out the principles of an open architecture to create personal computers before capital had come into the industry.' Felsenstein did not use 'hacking' in its most modern sense.

One of the conference's workshops, held in the old crypt beneath the Paradiso theatre, concerned security issues and intelligence services. The discussion was led by Stefen Wernery, Chaos' spokesman. He described how after the NASA hack in 1987 Chaos had tried to make contacts with the German secret service. 'We thought about what we could do so that nobody would get into trouble with the police and firms would also know their computers were secure. We decided to go to the secret service – the Verfassungschutz – about which systems had been hacked. We were worried that if we gave information to the German secret service the US Secret Service would know about it as well. That was a mistake; there's a lot of problems in exchange of information between the organisations. I had three meetings with the German service. They wanted me to work for them, but I refused.'

The German secret service was prepared to receive information and not insist on prosecuting, Wau Holland said. In America, John Draper pointed out, reporting a computer crime would result in the authorities opening a criminal file on you. 'The Secret Service in the US has a lot more power than the CIA or the FBI,' Draper alleged. Three or four years ago computer crimes were handled at state level locally. Those investigations are now done by the Secret Service.'

The situation in Europe was changing as well, Wernery warned. He said he had once believed police forces couldn't tell the difference between a toaster and a floppy disk, but many countries now had special computer crime departments working with their local PTTs (telephone authorities). 'The US agencies have a great desire to catch a German hacker and put him in prison.' But he doubted there was sufficient international co-operation. 'The problem is one country doesn't want to give the other country any information,' he said.

Hübner also posed the problem of knowing who one was dealing with on the networks. 'There's no easy way to tell if someone is a KGB agent,' he said. 'In our case, though, the contact was made by our side.' Giving information to the people was OK, Holland chipped in, giving it to the KGB was not.

Draper believed the problem was merely a matter of being careful: 'If someone asks me about something that's taboo technology, I'm very cautious. I say I must ask my supervisor or something. As trade restrictions ease the Russians will become part of the European Community eventually. We are going to get more and more people in the East on line.'

Hübner doubted that the secret services would be able to keep track of all hackers as the number of networks multiplied. Draper thought differently. 'The US Secret Service probably has a whole department which just monitors bulletin boards,' he suspected.

Circulating around the conference was a draft declaration for the International Conference on the Alternative Use of Technology. This asserted:

'The free and unfettered flow of information is an essential part of our fundamental liberties and shall be upheld in all circumstances.

'Governments shall be fully accessible to all people at all times. Information technology shall enhance the scope of this right, not reduce it.

'The protection of individual liberties being our paramount concern, we demand that no private information shall be stored and restored by electronic means.

'Once private data is banned from the realm of informatics [sic], all data therein and all networks shall be freely accessible. Repression and prosecution shall become devoid of sense.

'Computer technology shall not be used by government and corporation bodies to control and oppress the people.'

It is a charter for those worried by the image of Big Brother, his power enhanced by state-dominated information technology.

The Galactic Hacker Party inevitably attracted disapproving notices. Donn Parker, the American computer crime expert, claimed young people were being lured into hacking by a potent mix of idealism and science fiction. Hackers were becoming less mischievous and more militant, he told the Royal Aeronautical Society in London in September. He compared hackers, united by an emotive and idealistic cause, to the rise of international terrorism, *The Times* reported. 'He said that at the Galactic Hacker Party delegates stated their intent to make computers and the information they held freely accessible to the people.'

Later in August 1989, three West Germans were charged with spying for the Soviet Union. Hans Hübner was not one of them. The investigating authorities were satisfied that he had co-operated with them and had not passed any secrets or computer passwords to the East. The three charged were Markus Hess, who, it was alleged, had been traced back to Hanover by Stoll's SDInet decoy, Peter Carl, alleged to have been the middleman, and Dirk Brzezinski, a computer programmer. In early January

1990 the three went on trial in Celle, Lower Saxony. Among those called to give evidence was Dr Clifford Stoll.

An FBI agent accompanied him to West Germany. In the foyer of the courthouse, Stoll saw his electronic opponents in the flesh for the first time. 'I felt I knew these hackers already,' he said after he had given his evidence. 'But there were people watching me and I wanted to give my testimony without prejudice so I couldn't speak to him. I knew Hess from what he had typed into my computers. I had watched him for over a year.' Nonetheless Stoll's view of the West German hackers shifted during the trial. 'Hess appeared more human. I expected a much more mechanical person. Instead I found a real human being who was saying "Help, I'm in trouble here". I had talked to him before very briefly, via electronic mail, but it wouldn't have done to say very much then. When this is all over we are going to have to have a long talk about it.'

Did he hate the hackers? 'No. Not the people, but I hated their deeds. It wasn't so much the treachery to a nation, but the breach of trust. Our computers and computer networks form neighbourhoods. Now we have found out that communities of computer users have just the same sort of problems as every other neighbourhood. Most people are wonderful neighbours but a few people wreck it for others. There are bastards who will break into other's computers, steal information, invade privacy and sell it to the KGB. I believe our data banks and computers deserve respect.'

Stoll had no doubt that valuable defence secrets were passed to the Russians. Secreted in the mass of dud technical details assembled to set up SDInet was a letterhead giving an address for users to write to requesting more information. Several months after Hess had discovered the decoy network, a letter arrived at Lawrence Berkeley from an East Coast businessman known to have had dealings with Eastern bloc embassies. The FBI was still considering his case. 'I know they got a great deal of information. They stole files on US spy satellites which were due to be sent up on the shuttle. They were getting details about chemical and biological warfare plans for the Central European theatre of war. I saw the stuff going out directly to Hanover in West Germany.'

As for Koch's death, Stoll speculated there were many groups who could have wanted him dead. 'They never found a suicide note by his body. He was a distressed person, but there were cocaine dealers and others . . .'

The Cuckoo's Egg has become a bestseller in the States. The CIA presented him with a 'certificate of appreciation' for his spycatching work. And Stoll, who describes himself as a West Coast ex-hippy and a member of a three-bicycle household, has turned the focus of his attention back to astronomy. Hess, Brzezinski and Carl were convicted in February 1990. They all received suspended prison sentences.

IX

CRIMINAL, TRESPASSER OR
PUBLIC SERVANT?

British law has been slow to come to terms with the problems created by the spread of computers in society. The process has been more protracted than in other advanced industrialised states, reflecting either the poor lobbying power the computer industry is able to exert, the low priority accorded matters technological, or alternatively, a reluctance to be panicked into knee-jerk legislation.

Hacking is not an easy target for legislation. It raises wider issues about the freedom and ownership of information. Existing acts have been reinterpreted to cover novel computer-related crimes. The courts have not always taken kindly to this process of bending or extending laws. Erasing or amending information held on computers has generally been dealt with by criminal damage legislation. Using another's computer time without permission or making free calls on someone's account have led to charges of theft of electricity. Copying programs or information may come within the ambit of the copyright laws, while penetrating military or defence establishments could result in a prosecution under the Official Secrets Act.

This process of extending existing laws broke down, however, after the failure of the Forgery Act against Gold and Schifreen.

Breaking into a computer, overcoming its security procedures, investigating and leaving again, with no damage having been caused, remained legal. Many believe the mere act of gaining unauthorised access should not be criminalised. Nevertheless, by early 1989 there were growing demands that Britain should bring its laws into line with countries that had already made gaining unauthorised access an offence.

The debate on hacking, conducted chiefly through the workings of the Law Commission, has embraced other aspects of computer misuse, including deliberate computer fraud, electronic eavesdropping and the duty of companies to reveal when they have been hacked into. The discussions have raised many awkward issues. How does a prosecution prove those accused were responsible for damaging data in a computer if they were remote users, possibly thousands of miles away when the alleged crime was committed? And where such proof is obtained, what is to be done about a crime initiated in the Home Counties, for example, and perpetrated against systems in Japan, Europe or the United States? Who would have jurisdiction?

With the example of Edward Singh's exploits before them, and the moral panic over computer viruses at its height, many businesses and organisations have rapidly been coming round to the view that some legal sanction, however difficult to enforce, is necessary. If nothing else, it would serve as a timely warning to errant or overcurious teenagers.

As early as 1984, lawyers from the Scottish Law Commission in Edinburgh encouraged members of the Law Society of Scotland to request an examination of the legal aspects of the use and abuse of computers. Well ahead of their colleagues south of the border, the Commission published their provisional proposals in 1986. At that stage the best available data – not much more than an informed guesstimate – suggested computer-assisted fraud and theft were costing UK industry £40 million a year. A draft bill was circulated in 1987. This proposed criminalising hacking with prison terms of up to two years.

The Scottish Commission broke the subject down into eight categories of computer misuse. On obtaining unauthorised access to a computer, the report noted: 'Many who indulge in the activity of hacking, in the sense of obtaining remote access, are merely curious to test their electronic and technological skills and have no nefarious motive in mind.' It continued: '. . . the activity of hacking may give access to secret or confidential information which the hacker is not entitled to see and which the unscrupulous person may use to his own advantage.'

Four main reasons were then advanced for the need to criminalise simple hacking. 'Opportunities now exist for gaining access to private data which never existed before,' the report stated, 'without having to break into a building or an office to do so.' The potential danger arising from any one break-in was also higher. Increasingly elaborate and diverse information was now being collected and stored on computers and held at one point. Following the arguments advanced in the Data Protection Act of 1984, there was also the implication that in many cases unauthorised people should not be permitted 'with impunity to pry into another's affairs.' And lastly, the Scottish Commission argued, hacking may be the 'prelude to other activities such as fraud or theft, or the corruption of data or programs.'

Using telephone tapping – which is controlled by the Interception of Communications Act 1985 – as an analogy, the report suggested that access to a computer for official purposes not sanctioned by the system's owner would require a warrant. 'It would be unfortunate if the police or other investigating authorities were to be at risk of committing an offence by covertly accessing programs or data stored in a computer even when that was for the purpose of detecting or preventing serious crime.' Advice on such a clause had not been obtained from the security services at that stage. Three grounds for issuing a warrant were advanced: in the interest of national security; for preventing or detecting serious crime; or for the purpose of 'safeguarding the economic wellbeing of the United Kingdom.'

The Scottish Law Commission raised one other novel aspect of hacking. Having pointed out that there was little evidence of the true extent of damage done by computer fraudsters and hackers, it suggested that there could be a specific statutory duty for companies to disclose incidents of computer crimes which had affected them. Many companies which were hacked into were reluctant to publish the fact for fear of loss of business confidence in the integrity of their services. In favour of such a clause was the argument that non-disclosure by the victims encouraged criminals to 'have a go'. Keeping quiet about incidents also meant the need for reform could not be reasonably assessed and companies which should have taken extra precautions were being left vulnerable through a lack of publicity about the dangers. In the end the opposing arguments won. The final report concluded that imposing such a duty on the victim would raise a similar question for hundreds of other categories of crime. In practice, it would probably have been unenforceable. Although the Scottish Law Commission Bill was not enacted, concern about companies hushing up their vulnerability persisted.

In April 1988 the House of Lords removed the one act that until then the authorities had hoped could be used to prevent anyone gaining unauthorised access to computers. Five Law Lords unanimously upheld a Court of Appeal ruling that Steve Gold and Robert Schifreen were not guilty of forgery. It was a test case that had taken nearly three years to wind its way through the courts. In fact, both Schifreen, from Edgware in north London, and Gold, from Sheffield, were as much journalists as hackers. In mid-1984 Schifreen had told Gold he had discovered an ID and password belonging to a member of British Telecom's staff which gave free access to the Prestel computing service. Assuming the official's electronic identity allowed them to read areas of Prestel closed to ordinary users. These were administrative sections of the computer and they contained details of other files and services. One route they discovered eventually turned up a page which held the ID and password for the systems manager. This conferred on them the highest privileges within Prestel. They could obtain other passwords and alter information in files. Schifreen also found one of the more interesting electronic mailbox accounts on the system: that of the Duke of Edinburgh. There was virtually nothing in it, but to gain maximum publicity and prove he had hacked his way in, Schifreen left a number of messages in the mailbox. Most of the messages already there were, he told the court later, 'not very interesting'. They were mainly concerned with the birth of Prince William.

Gold and Schifreen told Micronet, one of the services using Prestel, how they had broken in, and Prestel was informed of the flaws in its security. Warned of the break-in, Prestel changed the passwords of those who provided information for the pages, but they were soon cracked again by Schifreen and Gold. Prestel's alteration had left most users with simple and predictable passwords. The system was penetrated once more. Again Prestel was informed of the weaknesses. By now not only Schifreen and Gold had obtained IDs and passwords; others too were exchanging them via chatlines on Prestel.

Prestel decided to use the law to make an example of what it considered to be two key hackers. Telephone taps were put on the line from Schifreen's home and messages exchanged between him and Gold were recorded. On 26 March 1985 police and British Telecom personnel raided both of their homes simultaneously. They were taken to Holborn police station, detained overnight, and told they were being arrested for hacking. The police officer in charge of the investigation was Detective Inspector John Austen. Gold and Schifreen were charged under the 1981 Forgery and Counterfeiting Act. When the case finally came to trial at Southwark Crown Court in 1986 they were convicted of nine offences. They were granted the right to fight the decision in higher courts and the Court of Appeal duly quashed the convictions. Lord Lane, one of the Appeal judges, ruled that the prosecution was an attempt to 'force the facts of the case into the language of an act not designed to fit them'. British Telecom counterappealed, but the House of Lords confirmed the Appeal Court's decision. (Although phone phreakers had previously been found guilty of theft of electricity, no such fall-back charge was used by the police to secure a conviction against Gold or Schifreen.)

The attempt to use the Forgery Acts as a means of criminalising the process of using someone else's electronic identity and password had failed. 'If hacking was to be considered a crime,' Gold wrote shortly afterwards, 'then a change in the law was required.' Schifreen went further: 'There are loopholes in our law and in everyday computer practices that are a threat to all of us.' He advocated the passing of a specific computer crime act, drafted in consultation with hackers, which would include making the use of another person's password and ID without permission a criminal offence. 'Those whose job it is to keep hackers away from computers must be taught to think like hackers and not like old-fashioned computer operators.'

In England the climate of opinion towards hacking began to change significantly during 1988. One of the contributory factors was the lack of any firm conclusion in the English Law Commission's Green Paper (No 110) on Computer Misuse published in August that year. The report had been delayed until the result of the Schifreen and Gold case was decided by the Law Lords. On the central issue of whether hacking should be criminalised or not, the Green Paper made no recommendation. It seemed as though the issue might take years to resolve.

Working paper No 110 declared: 'We make no provisional proposals on whether hacking should be an offence. Such conduct is not an offence at present, although it may in certain limited circumstances amount to an offence under the Data

Protection Act 1984.' If it should be decided to make gaining unauthorised access a criminal offence, the report continued, it should only be 'tryable in the magistrates courts and should not be punishable with imprisonment.' Nor should attempting to hack become an offence. The Commission's conclusions, outlining a number of options, swiftly came under attack from a wide range of interest groups.

At the same time the number of computer incidents reported began to multiply, aided by the panic associated with computer viruses. In July 1988 the potential £32 million computer fraud on the Union Bank of Switzerland was made public, and in October Edward Singh's arrest added to the growing concern of the financial and military establishments on both sides of the Atlantic. Then, in November, Robert Morris, a Cornell University student, managed to close down thousands of computers on the Arpanet service in the United States by releasing a worm program that reproduced itself across the networks, crashing hundreds of machines. By early 1989, the CBI raised its figure for the cost of computer incidents to British Industry to £400 million a year. Computer firms, financial institutions and many other organisations began to admit that there were weaknesses in networks and systems, and began calling for legal protection.

The Commission announced that new submissions should be sent to its offices by the end of February 1989 for the consideration of a White Paper on the subject of hacking. Many submissions arrived after the deadline but were accepted. One of the more damaging arguments for the Commission's working paper was advanced by the Data Protection Registrar. This disputed the contention that the Data Protection Act could be deployed in any useful way against hacking. Not all the submissions were in favour of criminalising hacking.

By the time the Forgery and Counterfeiting Act case against Gold and Schifreen had collapsed a substantial number of Western industrialised countries had already passed computer crime legislation. 'These include some of our major competitors,' the Confederation of British Industry warned in its submission to the Law Commission in February 1989. The United States of America, Canada, West Germany, Switzerland, Norway, Denmark and France all had anti-hacking statutes. 'We do not want the United Kingdom to be put at an economic disadvantage nor to become a haven for criminals. This may occur if our society is not adequately protected against computer misuse, especially when other countries do provide comprehensive computer legislation.' Other countries had formally amended existing laws to make unauthorised access to a computer illegal. These included the Australian state of Victoria, and Sweden.

In France, Article 462-2 of the Law 88-19 has provided an offence of fraudulent access to a machine. The offence even covers the eventuality of a computer user who inadvertently logs onto a wrong system or data base to which he is not entitled to have access and who fails to leave immediately. Another article, in the same code, gives wide powers to deem members of hacking clubs liable to charges of conspiracy and incitement. This provision was aimed at groups similar to the Chaos Computer Club, which the French authorities had come to loathe. Any group of students joining together to pool information would be in danger of being caught by this article, but the British CBI admired the effect of this clause. 'Hackers learn how to carry out their unauthorised activities by using electronic bulletin boards,' the CBI declared. 'We consider that some of these boards incite hackers by exchanging information about passwords and hacking techniques.' Such 'preliminary' acts should also be criminalised. The CBI submission further noted that a number of countries – West Germany, Switzerland, states in the USA, and Canada – provided extra legal protection for information held on computers. It urged the Law Commission to revive proposals from the 1981 Report on Breach of Confidence which allowed those who had taken the information to be sued for damages.

The Law Commission accepted that the overwhelming majority of countries which had considered the question concluded that some specific computer legislation was necessary. Only Belgium, Iceland and Japan had decided their existing laws were adequate. The Law Reform Commission of Tasmania, for example, said: 'Such legislation would make it no longer necessary for prosecutors to shoehorn cases into existing common law crimes . . . which acknowledge neither the complexity of computers nor the new types of undesirable activity which involve computers.' The Tasmanian Commission highlighted one shoehorning case where a Hong Kong computer technician was charged under a theft ordinance in relation to abstracting electricity for hacking into an electronic mailbox system. The electricity used was worth less than one-eighth of a Hong Kong cent. The court found him guilty but he was discharged after the magistrates declared the prosecution should never have been brought.

By contrast, the Computer Fraud and Abuse Act passed by the United States Congress in 1984 laid down maximum penalties of a fine up to $250,000 or twice the value of lost or damaged property, and ten years in prison for a first offence of simply attempting to enter a computer system illegally. More serious offences are liable to twenty years in jail. The Federal Computer Fraud Act only outlawed unauthorised access to certain categories of computer systems, mainly those used by federal government agencies. Unauthorised access to other systems without causing damage was not made illegal, but it was left to individual states to decide upon local regulations. The West German law of 1986 similarly made unauthorised entry into a select category of computers illegal, in this case it covered computers deemed to be 'secure'.

One of the earliest specific computer statutes was the state of Florida's Computer Crimes Act, passed in 1978. This used the concept of 'offences against intellectual property', which included modifying, destroying, disclosing or taking any data from a computer. By April 1987 every US state bar three — Arkansas, Vermont and West Virginia — had passed computer legislation. In California anyone who 'knowingly and without permission accesses or causes to be accessed any computer, computer system or computer network', faced up to one year in jail and a $5,000 fine. The Canadian Criminal Law Amendment Act of 1985 brought in the idea of 'mischief'. It declared that anyone commits a mischief who 'destroys or alters data; renders data meaningless, useless or ineffective; obstructs, interrupts or interferes with the lawful use of data; or denies access to data to a person who is entitled to access thereto.'

The Swedish Data Act of 1973 was the first to create an offence of merely gaining unauthorised access to a computer. Many other countries have since followed suit. Some American states have also criminalised unauthorised use of computer time. Employees who misuse a works computer in California are liable to prosecution if the cost of computer time and services exceeds $100. If the cost is below that sum and causes no damage then they would be dealt with under another law. Both the Californian law and the draft Israeli computer bill give powers for electronic equipment and software to be seized and forfeited.

As ever, the best of foreign practices were quoted by many companies in their submissions to the Law Commission in order to demonstrate that Britain was slow to react and out of step with the rest of the world. The UK was not entirely alone, however. Coopers and Lybrand in their study of network security for the Commission of European Communities, drew attention to the fact that Italy had 'no adequate regulations covering the damage, abuse, theft or destruction of a company's information'. Interception of computer communications was not an offence.

Why should computers enjoy special legal protection? The English Law Commission advanced numerous arguments for resisting the creation of a new crime. Although hacking might be an invasion of privacy, the working paper had explained, there was no such general offence in English law. Trespass is not a criminal action unless damage is done. Nor is information property under English law. There is no crime of industrial espionage. The problems of enforcement and the difficulties in detecting hackers meant the law might never be used and would fall into disrepute. If damage had been done to a system, criminal damage or fraud might be more relevant charges. The lack of publicised incidents up until that point suggested to the Commission there was not an 'impending crisis of a kind that demanded prompt legislative action.'

Support for these lines of reasoning came from many quarters. Alistair Kelman, the barrister who represented Gold and Schifreen, maintained there was no need for a new criminal offence of hacking. Under the Telecommunications Act 1984, he believed, hacking which involved avoidance of payment was already an offence. Search warrants could already be obtained for illegal extraction of electricity. The problem was partially administrative. British Telecom was getting better at telephone tracebacks and co-operation with authorities abroad would eventually develop. The onus for improving security lay with firms. 'If British Telecom had been complying with the law (specifically the Companies Act and the Data Protection Act) in keeping itemised accounts and implementing an adequate security system neither Schifreen nor Gold would have been able to hack the networks,' Kelman wrote in a submission to the Law Commission.

Hackers are also of use to the business world. 'To test the security of a dial-up service it is now common practice to use hackers. Dummy data is placed on the proposed system, various security measures are adopted, and then the telephone number of the system is written on a hacker's electronic board.' Lessons learned from how the hackers play around with the system are then incorporated in the firm's redesign of the product. 'The alternative to using hackers is to employ specialist consultants whose fees can be considerable.' Criminalising hacking would have two undesired effects: network and systems managers would become complacent because they would rely on the law rather than on improving security, and criminalised young hackers would be driven into the arms of organised crime. The latter effect would be something akin to the effect of Prohibition in the United States. Furthermore, the police need help from hackers in informing them about what is happening on the networks. 'Hackers are being made whipping boys for generally lax computer security,' he concluded.

Another opponent of criminalisation was Professor Glyn Emery, a member of the British Computer Society. In a letter to *The Times* in April 1989 he disassociated himself from colleagues backing a new law. 'To expose inadequate security, whether in a computer system or an airport, is to do a service to the community,' he wrote. 'Such a bill would be contrary to the spirit of the English Law which has always regarded the property owner as responsible for the security of his own property . . . Trespass is (with a few unhappy exceptions) a civil, not a criminal offence.'

The Data Protection Registrar, Eric Howe, was also opposed to criminalising hacking which caused no damage. Overzealous laws would encourage a false sense of security among computer users. 'You've only yourself to blame if your neighbours' cattle get into your unfenced fields,' he said at one stage. Not all systems deserved the same security designation. 'A more selective and cautious approach is appropriate,' Mr Howe suggested. 'One offence should be related to an intent on the part of the hacker to gain some advantage for himself or another, or to damage another person's interests. A second could arise when actual damage is caused to data or software.' But certain categories of computers, air-traffic control systems, hospital data bases and those which might affect the health or safety of individuals, should be fully protected by law. Any unauthorised access into those systems specified as sensitive by the Secretary of State would be illegal. 'Hacking may be a juvenile hobby . . . it is undesirable to criminalise juveniles or introduce young people to the criminal justice system unnecessarily.'

The debate on hacking seems in many cases to be conducted in the form of a competition to produce the most compelling analogies. Another member of the British Computer Society, Terence Wright, elaborated on the idea of trespass in an article in *The Guardian*: 'When a man climbed through a Buckingham Palace window and sat on the Queen's bed, he was not charged with an offence. Is no word of criticism due to those who leave windows open in their computers? What privileges does a computer require that are denied the Sovereign?' Peter Sommer, author of *The Hacker's Handbook* and *Data Theft*, argued that new laws abroad had done little to deter hackers. 'If there's an argument for a new law,' he stated, 'its centre should be not the medium upon which information is held but the classification of categories of data to be protected, the acts of unauthorised collection and transmission and whether there will be a public interest defence.' *The Guardian*'s computer editor, Jack Schofield, proposed a simpler solution. Every hacker should be paid a bounty of £100 for every break-in which exposed new weaknesses in companies' computer systems. The fines would soon convince firms to tighten up access.

Multinational computer companies and major corporations would not have been amused at the suggestion of paying hackers performance-related cash prizes. Deterring hacking is necessary, such organisations believe, otherwise society would be unable to rely on computers and would be inhibited in making full use of them. Making unauthorised access into an offence would strengthen the intention of the Data Protection Act. These are not marginal issues, such companies contend. The English Law Commission's first report had conceded that 'If the computer system disrupted was the air-traffic control computer at an airport the consequences might be disastrous. No computer system is completely secure.' The Commission suggested a new law might, if nothing else, serve as an important deterrent. It would 'signal society's disapproval of those who deliberately set out to breach security measures, and amount to a rejection of the claim that hacking is a harmless pastime.'

Under-reporting of incidents is inevitable, but it should not be used as an excuse for doing nothing, claimed those demanding action. 'Some victims certainly fear that revealing misuse incidents will only result in a loss of confidence which will further damage that organisation's interests,' IBM said. It would be quite unrealistic for data users to have legal obligations under the Data Protection Act 'whilst would-be intruders are free to attack systems without fear of penalty.' IBM urged the Commission to consider a computer password as similar to a lock and key, and that breaking through them was therefore the same as breaking and entering a house.

Some of the most practical arguments put forward were examples which underlined the fact that modern society is becoming more and more dependent on computers. 'We believe we cannot wait until there is a major disaster before appropriate legislation is enacted to bring the available legal remedies into line with the changes in information technology and its uses,' the CBI submission stated. 'Computers play a key role in the control of industrial processes (in chemical plants and nuclear reactors) and production equipment; in medical research and evaluation; and in the processing and storage of personal information.' The CBI document referred to the Lawrence Livermore National Laboratory in California, a centre for the design, manufacture and testing of nuclear weapons, which suffered $100,000 worth of damage. A hacker broke in through Internet, causing severe problems to the system. For a pharmaceutical company stolen research data could lead to loss of patent rights and cost millions of pounds, suggested the CBI. Computers, the organisation accepted, were not quite the business panaceas they had once been made out to be: 'Effective use of computers means that access to them must be widespread, while effective security means that access must be restricted.'

The British Computer Society put forward a number of disturbing scenarios: 'The risks to the public, state bodies and businesses cannot be quantified, but range from a Chernobyl-scale disaster, through the dangers of corrupted medical records, to the bankruptcy of commercial operations.' With the enlargement of computer networks the dangers have increased. Hacking could lead to loss of life. Radiation dosages in health-care systems might be tampered with, and disrupted road traffic-flow control systems could produce multiple pile-ups. Even the delay of data could have a powerful impact. 'There is an event on record involving the results of a horse race which were transmitted to a bookmaker's branch office after deliberate electronic delay so that a bet could be placed on the winning horse by the perpetrators.' Instead of deeming a computer to have a right to privacy, the law should rule that it had a right to have its integrity protected. The BCS called for 'intentionally attaining access to any computing system without authority' to be made a criminal offence 'under all circumstances'. And, it added, if the 'present situation of information having questionable status as property continues, it is likely to lead to great difficulty in detecting and enforcing any statutes relating to computer misuse'.

Digital, embroiled in the case of Kevin Mitnick, was convinced hacking was a serious threat to its business. Mitnick had been charged with stealing proprietary Digital security software valued at more than $1 million. The cost to the company in rewriting files and lost time was estimated at $4 million. Digital did not believe Mitnick was providing a public service.

For businesses, all the time spent repairing and checking is included in the final account of the damage caused to a computer system. According to IBM, in its submission to the English Law Commission in February 1989: 'Until the system has been comprehensively checked through, involving expert, lengthy and costly analysis, it cannot be fully restored to use. A bank or similar financial institution cannot afford to undertake financial transactions on a system which may contain incorrect data or viruses which could corrupt any such transactions. In this way the mere fact of an unauthorised access significantly damages a system for a significant period of time and necessitates substantial and costly corrective measures.'

Digital's submission to the English Law Commission included a sheaf of press cuttings of hacking cases and lists of network addresses and IDs taken from bulletin boards. Some scientists were so worried about the possibility of experimental data being stolen they were inhibited from using networks for their research, Digital maintained. Bulletin boards came in for fierce attack. 'Hacking conferences can be likened to conferences in which there are lectures on the latest ways of picking locks and short-circuiting burglar alarms.' The potential for damage was enormous in nuclear power plants, missile warning systems, air-traffic control centres, railway signalling systems, medical monitoring and financial records. Unauthorised access is already the subject of special acts and bylaws in other areas; it is an offence in certain areas of railway tracks and airports, for example: 'Any failure to outlaw hacking is akin to allowing members of the public to wander across runways at Heathrow.' Digital accepted there was no such thing as perfect computer security, but believed some anti-hacking law was necessary to enforce what precautions could be taken. 'Clearly hackers derive enjoyment from the activity. However this is the case with many forms of criminal activity which are nevertheless forbidden because they are harmful.' Digital was so exercised by the growing legal problems associated with computers that later in 1989 it endowed a chair in Information Technology Law at the Queen Mary and Westfield College, University of London.

Although hacking is the most bitterly contested element of the computer misuse debate, other deficiencies of the law relating to new technology have also come under attack. Even the 1988 English Law Commission's working paper recognised that statutes were outdated in the area of fraud. The notion of deception, for example, could not be applied to a computer. Only human beings could be deceived. An amendment to the Theft Act was therefore suggested, allowing deception to include 'Inducing a machine to respond to false representations, which the person making them knows to be false, as if they were true.' In 1981 a judge at Acton Crown Court, west London, had ruled that the computer processing of VAT returns which had been encouraged to pay out false returns presented no satisfactory evidence for the case to be put to a jury. A new amendment would cover such cases. The vast majority of fraud cases involving machines also required a person to be deceived at some stage, so were already covered by the current law. Several computer payroll frauds had been noted. In one, a housing benefits clerk claimed fraudulent payments for his brother-in-law. £12,000 was paid into building society accounts, but the clerk was apprehended and prosecuted. Another involved a wages clerk who programmed extra overtime claims for a workforce and then split the proceeds fifty-fifty with them. They too were caught. Sixteen people were charged after losses amounting to £54,000 over three years were discovered.

Damage to computer software became accepted as a criminal damage offence as late as 1986, following a test case (Cox v Riley) which was taken up to the Divisional Court. This is one area where the law seems to have advanced by interpretation. A plastic circuit card containing the program that controlled a computer-operated saw was erased by an employee. The cost of reprogramming the card was said to be £620. The defendant was convicted at the magistrates court under the 1971 Criminal Damage Act. He appealed, but the conviction was upheld in the higher courts. The ruling implied that although the law did not recognise information as property, if it was stored on floppy disk or magnetic tape then it could be deemed to have been damaged. Hackers deliberately causing any alteration to data, or being reckless to such damage occurring, could therefore be prosecuted for criminal damage. There were still a few areas of doubt, the Commission conceded, for example where a hacker inadvertently activated security procedures which shut down a machine. The CBI was less than happy on relying on largely untested legal remedies and urged the Commission to consider modifying the 1971 Act to allow property to be defined as including computer programs and data.

Electronic eavesdropping on a computer – by picking up radio emissions given off from the monitor of a computer screen – was deemed to be outside the remit of Commission's brief. Eavesdropping only allowed the listener-in to view what was on the screen at any one time, on a similar principle to that operated by TV detector vans. But this did not prevent several organisations, including the CBI, calling for the principle of unauthorised access to be extended to eavesdropping.

The Law Commission also excluded the rules of evidence from its study. A number of submissions called for the simplification of the process for fear that an anti-hacking law would be almost unenforceable. Under the Police and Criminal Evidence Act, every time a computer print-out is produced in court it requires a witness to swear that the document was produced by the computer when there were no reasonable grounds for believing the machine was malfunctioning. Print-outs should be acceptable as direct evidence, it was claimed. The issue raises many difficulties. If a hacker disturbs a machine, might it not be claimed that the printing or other functions had also been upset? A full review of the rules of evidence seems inevitable at some stage when hacking becomes an offence.

The question of jurisdiction has also been recognised as raising further awkward legal problems. Once again, the Law Commission's working paper made no firm recommendations. It accepted that committing an offence abroad, through remotely interfering with a computer overseas while sitting in this country, could not be tried in Britain. For example, in the early 1980s, a telex operator employed at a Swiss bank in London had diverted money from an account in New York to another in Geneva which had been opened by a colleague. Many of those in favour of criminalising hacking also wanted to adopt new rules on jurisdiction. The New Zealand Crimes Act of 1961 has often been quoted as an example. The Act allows anyone who commits any part of the offence – which might include using a computer terminal to access networks – in the native country to be tried in the same country, even though the main part of the crime has been perpetrated elsewhere. In the case of Kevin Mitnick, one of the charges he faced in the US was for gaining illegal access to computer information held by Leeds University. Singh's case also raised fresh concerns in this area. According to the CBI: 'The case of computer enthusiast Edward Singh, who gained access to the National Aeronautics and Space Administration computer and an American nuclear weapons research centre, clearly illustrates the necessity' for an extension of jurisdiction.

The complications aroused by the international nature of hacking are highlighted by an embarrassing incident which occurred in March 1988. Steffen Wernery, the Chaos Computer Club's official spokesman, was arrested at Paris airport along with Hans Gliss, the editor of the computer security newsletter, *Datenschutz-Berater*. Both had been due to speak at the Securicom conference on hacking. The arresting authorities, the Brigade Financière, held Gliss for a day, but Wernery remained in a French cell for sixty-six days. The French police had for a long time been concerned about the penetration of computers holding sensitive information on military projects, and a number of electronic break-ins had been recorded at French military sites over the previous three years. After the announcement of the NASA hack, both the French and the West German police had suspected Chaos members of being responsible. Wernery's and Holland's apartments had been raided in September 1987, but the German police, after a three-month investigation, eventually cleared both of them of involvement. French suspicions, however, had lingered.

For Gliss, who had contacts with German intelligence services, the arrests came as a complete surprise. 'In Germany I'm invited; in France I'm arrested for information,' he remarked a year after his detention. 'The French took the matter very seriously. I was questioned. I wasn't used to be treated in that way. I had strong 'flu as well. It was embarrassing, I wasn't allowed to go to my hotel. The French police thought they finally had the opportunity for squeezing Wernery, whom they hadn't been able to talk to in Hamburg. I had the impression the police were just trying to find their way in a misty environment. Philips and Thomson had had sensitive information on their Vax machines. Wernery came at the right time to act as scapegoat. On the second day they held him they were told by the Hanover police that he had nothing to do with the case. They took another sixty-four days to find out they could not charge him with anything.' Gliss managed to prove his credentials to the French police and was released after a day. He attended Securicom, where he delivered Wernery's speech to the conference.

Among hackers, the ethical dilemma of their activities and the consequences do not go entirely undebated. Put in the most romantic way, some have images of themselves as Robin Hood figures. They are, in their own eyes, defenders of democracy, alerting the world to the inadequacies of computer systems and the misdeeds of multinational companies and governments in the field of information technology. Many hackers are concerned by the extraordinary concentration of information, and with it increased power, that computers have conferred on the modern state.

In a lengthy editorial in the spring 1989 edition of *2600*, the magazine considered the growing number of 'busts' and prison sentences meted out to hackers in the US. The piece summarises many of the arguments against criminalisation:

Our nation's brightest kids are being imprisoned for being a little too inquisitive. And that's a frightening thought. Judges should consider what actually took place and forget about the fact that computers were involved. Would it even be a crime if computers weren't involved? And what about intent? . . . Much can be learned from what the hacker uncovers. While hackers are far from being knights in shining armor, the notion of their being criminals is so far from the truth that it's almost funny. These are kids doing what kids have done for all time. The only difference here is that now they've learned how to use a tool, there will be many more abuses. Not just abuses *of* the tool. Abuses *by* the tool. That's where the real danger is. Hacking is not wrong, hacking is healthy. Hacking is not the same as stealing. Hacking uncovers design flaws and security deficiencies. Above all else, hacking proves that the ingenuity of a single mind is still the most powerful tool of all. We are hackers. Call us co-conspirators, fellow anarchists, whatever you want. We intend to keep learning. To suppress this desire is contrary to everything that is human. Like the authors who rose to defend Salman Rushdie from the long arm of hysteria, we must rise to defend those endangered by the hacker witch-hunts.

The idea that 'information must be free' dominated the early aims of Chaos, according to Hans Gliss. 'Information is part of social structure, so it was thought,' he said, 'if certain information was accessible for those who had the money, those who did not have the means to pay would be excluded.' Chaos has since refined its beliefs. Some information, the Club accepts, should be private.

But John Draper had a more practical objection to the

criminalisation of hacking. 'Once I got thrown into jail I had phone phreak classes,' he told the Galactic Hackers' Party in Amsterdam. 'I got physically abused. These prisoners said you better teach us or else. So we had lessons three times a week. Jails are colleges of crime. You get exposed to drugs. I could have been teaching dealers how to break into the Drug Enforcement Agency computer. They wanted to know how to monitor police radios and unscramble them and how to make untraceable phone calls. If they put hackers in jail they are asking for trouble. These people could be used by terrorists.' The time in jail was not entirely wasted, Draper admitted. 'While I was there I wrote the "Easy Writer" program for Apple Computers. That went up the hit parade and I lived off it for six years.'

The English Law Commission had just begun to consider the pile of submissions it had solicited for its white paper when a backbench Conservative MP, Emma Nicholson, announced her intention of introducing a private member's bill. Miss Nicholson was not without influence or experience. She had been a vice-chairwoman of the Conservative Party and before entering parliament had been a systems programmer and analyst with Britain's biggest computer company, ICL. Nicholson had become involved in the hacking debate before, when the British Computer Society had approached her over the Copyright Bill. She introduced an amendment to outlaw hacking in respect of copyright protection. The English Law Commission was, in her opinion, in danger of taking years to make up its mind. A bill of some sorts, even if only a stopgap measure, was necessary to stem the growth in hacking.

Her early day motion in the Commons stated: 'This House recognises with the deepest concern the rash of unauthorised invasions by outside parties of government and business computer files on mainframe systems.' There were 'potential threats to national security' unless the matter was legislated

BEATING THE SYSTEM

upon. The motion attracted support from both sides of the House, including Labour's technology spokesman, Jeremy Bray. The Nicholson bill was no half-hearted measure. Section two proposed a sentence of up to ten years' imprisonment for those convicted of gaining unauthorised access to a computer to their own or another's advantage or another's prejudice. Anyone without 'lawful authority or reasonable excuse' who had in their possession anything with the intention of effecting unauthorised access to their advantage or another's prejudice, would be liable to a five-year sentence. This last clause led many to believe that Nicholson was in effect arguing for the licensing of modems. Simple unauthorised access without malice would be dealt with by way of a fine. Her bill gave the police powers to issue warrants, monitor electronically transmitted data and destroy confiscated machinery. She proposed an enlargement of the notion of jurisdiction, permitting an offence where any part of the communication links were in England or Wales to be tried in this country.

Her hard-line approach had the support of many groups, including the CBI, whose submissions to the English Law Commission had urged immediate action. 'Earlier this century the legislation covering transport by horse and cart had to be altered, late and under pressure, to recognise the advent of the motor car,' Nicholson wrote in *The Guardian*. 'The lawyers now arguing from the lofty intellectual heights for freedom of all information base their thinking on the security needs of quill-pen records. Electronic stored information is the New World's gold and needs different measures of protection.' To further her anti-hacking campaign, she helped set up a hotline with the accountants Touche Ross to encourage companies to report incidents.

There followed a sustained output of stories and cautionary tales on the effects of hacking and the damage it was causing. At a succession of one-day conferences on computers, Nicholson was the guest speaker, expounding the problems caused by

172

hacking. The Open University wrote to her expressing support. With 11,000 students having access to personal computers, their systems now had to be heavily 'policed' to prevent hackers from getting in. Herbert and Sons, manufacturers of weighing equipment, revealed, through Nicholson, that someone had copied a new software package and sent it to a competitor. The development on the software was worth £160,000 but there was no legal redress for theft of the information. Scotland Yard's Computer Fraud Squad was also said to be in support of Nicholson's bill.

A dossier, compiled by Nicholson with the active help of the CBI, was handed to the Prime Minister in April. It contained approximately 100 cases of fraud, computer damage and industrial espionage. Many of the leading computer companies wrote letters to *The Times*. John Boyd, of Digital's legal department, declared: 'A change in the law won't be the complete answer any more than it is to other kinds of crime, but it will signal a change in the view society takes.' Later the same month, MPs at Westminster were provided with a computer display, organised by the CBI, to demonstrate the dangers of hacking. 'Bulletin boards, which hackers use to pass information to each other, will be featured,' the CBI promised. 'Hacking has now become a major international problem. The French and the Germans have already outlawed it, but we fear it may be 1992 before the UK gets around to banning it, unless urgent action is taken along the lines urged by Emma Nicholson.'

There was some opposition to the publicity campaign. Peter Sommer, in several newspaper articles, claimed that most of the cases in Nicholson's file were already tryable under existing offences. But there were several signs that the campaign was having an effect. The issue was passed by the Prime Minister to the Home Secretary for active consideration. Shortly afterwards, Douglas Hurd indicated that the final English Law Commission report would be brought forward to September and that hacking was likely to be criminalised. Nicholson's bill was finally withdrawn on its second reading in the belief that government legislation would follow in that autumn's Queen's Speech. Over the summer responsibility for hacking was transferred to the Department of Trade and Industry.

The English Law Commission's final report on computer misuse was published on 10 October 1989, and was hailed as a victory for the anti-hacking camp. Three new criminal offences were proposed in order to deal with unauthorised access into a system, whether or not damage was caused. Unauthorised access without affecting the system would be liable to three months' imprisonment, while access with intent to commit a serious crime (for example attempting to manipulate electronic funds transfer systems), and access which altered data or programs (for example using worms, viruses or logic bombs) would both carry a penalty of five years in prison. The Law Commissioner, Richard Buxton, QC, reported: 'The basic offence is intended to deter what is a widespread activity by making it clear that hacking . . . is no longer acceptable. We have been careful to ensure that the offences catch only those who deliberately misuse computers and not persons who are merely careless or incompetent in their use of computers.'

But the Commission pointed out that if their proposals were enacted a gap remained in the law covering computer-based fraud initiated in England and Wales and completed abroad. In the report the Commission quoted several examples to illustrate the growing extent of the problem. One hacker, it recounted, had entered a university computer system and erased the results of two years' scientific experiments. In another case a British hacker had broken into an American computerised mail-ordering company and added large numbers of new names in the UK to the mailing list. Hacking had become endemic to the world's electronic networks, the Commission accepted. Electronic eavesdropping, though, was deemed to be a far lesser problem and left out of the recommendations.

But before the end of the same month the anti-hacking lobby suffered a sharp setback. The Government decided that its political timetable was so tight it could not afford the time in the 1989–90 parliamentary session. Nicholas Ridley, the Secretary of State for Trade and Industry, had welcomed the new Law Commission proposals. He had not, however, been convinced of the urgency of the matter. Nicholson told *The Times*: 'I am very concerned that the key minister, who has not been brought up in a computer environment, may not have grasped fully the fearsome nature of computer terrorism.'

Intense lobbying followed in an attempt to persuade the Government to include an anti-hacking bill in the Queen's Speech. *The Times*, the paper with the least doubts about the virtue of criminalising hacking, thundered forth with a leader condemning Government inaction: 'Computer hacking needs to be treated as a crime,' it stated. 'Three days after the Law Commission's study, the computer world cringed before the threat of a Friday-the-thirteenth virus. The predicted plague did not materialise – quite. But this was partly because industry was forewarned and took preventive action . . . The value of data stored on disk is now such that the need to protect it is a matter of national importance.'

A lobby of parliament by companies eager for a change in the law was arranged. One of the consultants to the Law Commission, Jeffrey Chapman, spoke out on the subject: 'One assumes that the reluctance to legislate is a reflection of the Cabinet's collective ignorance on this issue.' But the agitation was to no immediate avail. No anti-hacking measure appeared in the Queen's Speech. The Department of Trade and Industry described the legislation as too complicated and time-consuming, but it promised to support any MP who introduced a private member's bill along the lines of the Law Commission report. The lobbying eventually had its effect. After the draw for places in the order of private members' bills, Michael Colvin, the Conservative MP for Romsey and

Waterside, announced that he would introduce computer abuse legislation. He claimed that computer crime was costing Britain £2 billion a year. 'This measure is so urgent it cannot afford to wait for another year,' he said in December 1989. 'I still have to identify precisely where the opposition to it lies other than in the criminal fraternity.'

In a letter to *The Times* at the end of December, Miss Nicholson said she was 'delighted' that Michael Colvin had picked up the proposed legislation. And she redefined her stereotype of the hacker: 'I have been told,' she said, 'by security sources that extremists in Holland and Germany have used computer-derived information to bomb oil refineries and have destabilised government actions. With such a background, no special case consideration can be retained for the hacker. Those innocents who claim immunity must realise that they stand in the company of the international terrorist and industrial blackmailer.'

In February 1990, Nicholson announced her intention of tabling a series of amendments to the bill which would make computer evidence admissible in court and give greater powers to the police in obtaining search warrants and access to computers. Colvin was reported to be dismayed at the prospect of matters which might distract MPs from the 'simplicity of the basic offence'. His bill was given an unopposed second reading later that month. At the time of going to press it seems likely that hacking, in the form of obtaining unauthorised access, will be illegal by the summer of 1990.

Several weeks after the Queen's Speech, 150 computer experts and lawyers gathered in the lofty surroundings of the House of Commons' Committee Room 14, high above the Thames. Beneath a panorama of the defeat of the Spanish Armada, the British Computer Society's Law Specialist Group debated the motion that 'This house considers hacking should be a criminal offence'. Nicholson was opposed by Professor Bryan Niblett, also of the BCS. 'The Law Commission's first working paper was flabby in the extreme,' Nicholson declared. 'It dismissed too many hacking cases as media hype and media scare. The subsequent report vindicated their reputation.' Some information, such as personal health and individual bank accounts, has a right to be kept private. 'I don't believe we wish to create a global village where there are no boundaries at all.'

Professor Niblett reminded the audience that trespass was a tort, 'a wrongful thing', a civil matter not a criminal offence. Industry wanted the benefits of computers without the burdens. There had been widespread complacency over computer security and only belatedly was that beginning to change. One member of the audience suggested that hackers should be paid a substantial fee for the risks they ran in unearthing security weaknesses. A Scottish lawyer deplored the English law's obsession with 'word games'. As early as 1777, he explained, a Mr Dewar had been found guilty of an 'unnominate crime' for accessing one of his master's locked books. To another debater it was ironic to watch the Iron Curtain collapse as Britain considered another restriction on freedom of information. Was the hacker a trespasser or a housebreaker? At the end of the debate, on a show of hands, the vote was narrowly in favour of criminalisation.

Several weeks after being arrested, Edward Singh had sat in the snug of a pub in the Surrey village of Godstone, considering similar matters. 'Making it illegal won't change the situation at all,' he had ventured in between sips of bitter. 'The problem lies with the systems administrators. But I agree I have done wrong. Basically, hacking should be outlawed.'

X

Hacking into the Future

In *The Mighty Micro*, the computer scientist Christopher Evans speculated on the future impact of the computer revolution on society. In many cases his predictions – made in 1979 – were somewhat overoptimistic. For example, he forecast a far shorter working week by the mid-1980s, the paper-free office, a massively improved education system, and the abolition of the front-door key. Many of his predictions about the applications of electronic technology in the 1990s were, however, startlingly accurate. Evans foresaw the miniaturisation of computers, the decline of mainframes, the facility of debiting personal accounts directly from shops, electronic tagging and the rapid growth – with the help of satellite links – of computer networks. The suppliers of that technology were to be the new leaders of industry. He believed that IBM would displace General Motors from the number-one position in *Fortune* magazine's Top 500 companies. In the event, IBM was the most profitable company in 1989, although it's overall profit figures have been slipping. General Motors was deemed to be the largest company in terms of sales turnover.

For several years now, as Evans suggested, the telecommunication networks have been impingeing on the consciousness of the layperson's world. He or she can use a computer at home, not only for typing letters and playing computer games, but also for shopping or home banking (to instruct the bank to send a cheque book or debit an account). The potential for exploiting these developments has become more and more evident. The 1990 film, *Rosalie goes Shopping*, was a popular and quirky portrayal of a woman who cannot stop spending. Her mounting debts encourage her to take up hacking and computer fraud with her home computer.

The Mighty Micro envisaged an increasing dependence on networks among financial and state institutions needing to store and retrieve burgeoning quantities of sensitive information. The book realised the potential vulnerabilities inherent in networks and their possible manipulation by criminals or political activists. Evans saw that more and more criminals would attempt to make use of the technology. As the general population became more adept at using computers, so too would criminals. 'One very real possibility is that criminals who realise the increasing dependence of police forces on data handling and processing machines will make every kind of effort to disrupt police computer networks,' Evans wrote. 'With a bit of ingenuity a criminal could arrange to feed the police network with misleading information, deflecting attention from planned criminal exercises or fouling up counter measures . . . Attempts to erase police records or introduce erroneous information will be even more common.' There was also mention of obsessions with computer games and calculators, and an exploration of the implications for the mental development of children. But of today's curious, technically skilled explorer of computer networks there was no hint.

Emerging from the technical advances that computers have brought us, is the question of who has right of access to the information stored on disks, tapes and electronic memories. The concentration of that information – through the computer's ability to assemble, sort, cross-reference, select and distribute data – has brought the vision of an omniscient, and therefore all powerful, state ever closer. In December 1989 Emma Nicholson was confronting the issue in much the same way as the Chaos Computer Club when she voiced concern over computerised information in the National Health Service. Who owned a patient's medical history, she wanted to know? The Department of Health believed it belonged to the doctor, but Treasury department solicitors countermanded the decision and declared it was NHS property. The question of whether information was capable of ownership was not sufficiently clear in English law, she concluded.

The National Health Service is currently in the process of installing extensive networks. General practitioners' records are being computerised and linked up on line to hospitals. The issue which Nicholson had referred to was, by late 1989, threatening the whole timetable of NHS computerisation. Many doctors had been accepting gifts of free computers from data processing companies in exchange for medical records. The processing companies were then selling the information on to drug companies for market research purposes. Patients' names and addresses were removed from the information by the time the records reached the drug companies. Although the scheme had been supported by the then Department of Health and Social Security since 1987, Treasury solicitors two years later were beginning to have doubts over the ethics of the exchanges. They disputed the claim that the information was the intellectual property of GPs. There were accusations that handing over the information involved breaches of confidentiality.

Computer safety has as a consequence become an ever more important concern during the 1980s, an area to which the Government has been forced to allocate increasingly substantial resources. The 1984 Data Protection Act was an attempt to resolve some of the problems raised by the spread of computerisation through society. The Data Registrar's full powers came into force in November 1987, but few people appeared to take advantage of the right to check personal information held about them. In March 1988, Government departments released figures for the first four months in which the Act had been in force. The DHSS, which made no charge for inquiries, had expected 20,000 requests a year, but had received only 270. The Home Office had been sent just sixteen requests.

Under the Act, individuals are given the right to ask for all information held on them except that kept for the purposes of detecting or preventing crime, catching or prosecuting offenders, and assessing or collecting tax. 'Computers . . . can help you get the goods you want and can lead to better services, by improving medical care or helping the police fight crime', the Data Protection Registrar's pamphlets explain. 'But the growth of computerised record-keeping brings dangers. Information may be entered wrongly or get out of date. Or it may be mixed up with someone else's. The effects can be serious. Individuals may be refused jobs, housing, benefit or credit, or overcharged for goods or services or even wrongfully arrested.' Anyone can object to the manner in which organisations collect or use personal data. In March 1989 the Registrar, Eric Howe, warned credit companies about the practice commonly known as 'red-lining', whereby finance companies refuse credit to individuals according to their address. Poor council estates are often said to be 'red-lined'. Howe demanded companies find ways of assessing credit-worthiness other than by address, and warned them that they were already in breach of the Data Protection Act. The Act, however, created the anomaly that records kept on paper are not subject to scrutiny.

Security problems such as these have increased as more and more information is being loaded onto computers which are in turn being networked in order that the information may be more widely used. Internationally, computer reliability has become a matter of greater concern. In 1989, members of the International Electrotechnical Commission set out a new standard for safety-critical systems used in civil aviation and hospitals. In 1987 the National Audit Office warned that data stored on existing computer systems was increasingly ill-protected and open to abuse. The four areas of security risk were said to be: loss of data through fire, floods or industrial action; errors in data that left unreliable records; abuse of information by staff leading to fraud, theft and unauthorised disclosure; and abuse from outsiders through terrorism, illegal infiltration or hacking. The report said that despite these risks there was no evidence of any abuse of information. But the following year, the Public Accounts Committee noted little improvement in the level of risk and reported there had already been eleven cases of computer fraud in Whitehall, mostly at the Department of Employment.

A code of practice for computer security, sponsored by the Department of Trade and Industry, was introduced in 1989 to be the equivalent of the US Department of Defense's *Orange Book* system. It was compiled by the Commercial Computer Security centre based at the Royal Signals and Radar Establishment at Malvern. The RSRE was also involved in developing with GPT Data Systems a range of 'highly secure' communication processors. The security evaluation of the new processors was carried out by the Computer and Electronic Security Group of the Government Communications Headquarters in Cheltenham. In fact, several sections of Britain's extensive intelligence community are responsible for computer affairs. There is the Electronic Security Committee, which oversees the protection of sensitive information held on computers and transmitted through networks, whilst a significant proportion of GCHQ's work is computer related; one division of the signals intelligence section deals exclusively with computer services. MI5 is reputed to use two large ICL systems capable of holding twenty million files.

The Government's own Data Network (GDN) was one of the

larger networks created in the 1980s. Overseen by the Government's Central Computing and Telecommunications Agency, the construction and management of the Whitehall network was put out to private tender. The Civil Service unions objected to a private company running the Service. To allay public fears it was announced that private contractors working on the GDN would be 'positively and negatively vetted' by the security services to prevent unauthorised use of personal information. *The Guardian* reported in 1987 that: 'The amount of information carried on the system is expected to grow by ten per cent every year for the first five years.' Among those who expressed concern about the GDN was the Data Protection Registrar, who pressed the Government to publish the rules governing the transfer of information between Whitehall departments. But the contract was won by Racal and the system became operational in January 1989. The GDN, linking offices all over the country, connects fourteen government departments, including the Home Office, the Departments of Health and Social Security, the Inland Revenue, and Customs and Excise. The Police National Computer is not joined in. The GDN is sealed off from outside connections and, according to Racal, can only be accessed from computers on government premises. One of the specifications was that no department should be able to have access to other departments' systems. Racal maintains it has had no evidence of abuse within the network. Access is regulated by computer location as well as ID and password.

Meanwhile the Department of Social Security has for several years been attempting to connect up all its local offices in a single computer system. The current estimate for the whole project is £2 billion. The scheme has been bedevilled by the sheer scale of the project and the complexity of Social Security rules. At one stage staff in Crosby, Merseyside, walked out for twenty-four hours in protest at the 'inefficient' computers on trial in their offices.

At the same time, new and highly complex data bases are

being created for hundreds of local authorities. Software packages for sensitive subjects have become more common means of distributing information. In early 1990, the Department of Health announced that it would supply council social work departments with packages containing expert research and guidelines on child abuse. In the aftermath of the Cleveland child abuse affair, the Government felt that many departments lacked relevant information to carry out their tasks effectively.

The Ministry of Defence is also setting up networks throughout its units to improve internal communications and budgeting, and under the long-winded title of 'A strategy for Non-operational Information Technology in the Ministry of Defence', the survey makes several pointed remarks on security. 'The skills and technology to assess, implement and evaluate security requirements in IT systems are still immature and incomplete,' the booklet observes. 'Security requirements can have a profound effect upon the cost, implementation timescale, functionality and indeed practicality of computer systems. Costs and timescales can be two or three times more for a classified system than an unclassified one. This is because of the additional cost of security devices, security evaluation and the computer processing overheads of maintaining security logs, security labelling and controlling access.'

Beyond local and national government, private firms, organisations, banks, hotels, and hundreds of groups are busily multiplying the number of on-line networks and data bases. Travel agents are connected up to airlines and tour operators. Supermarkets' stocking and ordering systems are linked to warehouse computers. Tesco has begun a pilot project for a computerised shopping service where customers can key in their shopping lists from home. Many professions have access to burgeoning subject-specific data bases. Journalists use World Reporter, an electronic library of newspaper cuttings which locates key words and names out of millions of items. Lawyers can refer to Lexis, whose computer data base is located in Dayton, Ohio, to extract both British and American law reports.

Environmental, human rights and peace groups have established their own data and communication networks. The largest grouping of these is the Association for Progressive Communications (APC). Through the Association, GreenNet in Britain is connected to Peacenet and Econet in the USA, Alternex in Brazil, the Web in Canada and FredsNaetet in Sweden. GreenNet's stated objective is: 'To provide to organisations working for the environment, peace, human rights and sustainable development movements, a communications capability as good as that available to the Government, military and multinationals.' The network has facilities for electronic mail, computer conferences and data bases. On Peacenet, American citizens can check up on the voting records of their representatives in Congress. Computers, the APC admits, were initially seen as manifestations of a repressive state: 'In 1963 student activists in Berkeley set an anti-computer tone to radical politics when they wore "Do not fold, spindle or mutilate" signs on their foreheads. For the next two decades computers were seen as a tool more for oppression than activism.'

GreenNet, founded in 1985 and funded partially by the Joseph Rowntree Charitable Trust, has shared offices with Friends of the Earth in London. Among the testimonials listed in its literature GreenNet includes one from the US Major General John Sinlaub. 'The demonstrators might have been part of Peacenet, a computer-linked network that can mobilise protesters nationwide,' he wrote in *Phoenix* magazine. 'Peacenet was responsible for demonstrations launched on college campuses when US troops were sent to Honduras. This gives you some idea of the forces working against us.'

As for the 1990s and beyond, Christopher Evans believed that developments in artificial intelligence would eventually result in robot-like, ultra intelligent machines (UIMs), and the nature of computing would undergo a second revolution. In fact work on artificial intelligence, known as the fifth and sixth generations of computers, is advancing rapidly. Some believe that it will be the software of these future generations which will kill off the hacker, albeit not for another twenty or even thirty years.

Researchers and developers into fifth-generation systems aim to build computers which appear to behave like the human mind, employing parallel processing techniques. At present fifth-generation programs are in their infancy. Expert systems, large data bases of specialised knowledge programmed to follow a set of instructions, have been one beginning of the quest for artificial intelligence. For example, there are already medical expert systems in existence which can diagnose the cause of abdominal pains. They reach their conclusion by asking the patient questions and processing the information. Doctors help refine and tweak the system as it is being developed. However, although they have been more successful than general practitioners in tests, mistrust by patients means a second opinion is always sought from a human doctor. Other expert systems include translation machines and programs for engineering diagnostics.'

The Japanese made the most noise in the development of this new generation of technology when they launched a multi-billion-yen project at the beginning of the 1980s to build an intelligent computer to be used in all walks of Japanese life within ten years. Their goal was to flood Japanese society with such machines and thereby take the pressure off the country's ageing population. But we are already in the 1990s and Japan has been forced to tone down its enthusiasm and reassess its technological goals. Japanese researchers have made impressive advances with multi-parallel hardware and within software, but so far they have been unable to combine the two successfully in a fifth-generation machine.

The fifth-generation computer is not built to think and reason like a human being, it merely gives the impression of doing so. Scientists of the sixth generation, on the other hand, wish to build computers which can reason. To do this they are redesigning hardware and software from scratch, rather than basing it on earlier technologies. Some are using biological techniques such as neural computing, which aims to develop systems that imitate the neurons of the human brain; others are developing new programming structures and languages. One of the world's leading experts in artificial intelligence is Professor Donald Michie of the Turing Research Institute in Glasgow, a codebreaker who worked alongside Alan Turing at Bletchley Park during the Second World War. He and his colleagues are working on developing robot technology which operates like a human rather than with the machine-like repetition of rigid pre-programmed tasks. Michie's robots would be able to learn through experience, and be able to adapt. One example he gives would be that of a robot which could continue riding a bike after one of the pedals had fallen off. A human being would improvise, but the types of robot machines now in existence would be unable to act beyond their set roles and crash the bicycle. Such major advances, Michie concedes, will take decades.

Redesigned computer languages – if that is what they will still be called – for the sixth generation would be better structured and therefore cleaner, Michie believes. 'The present software landscape is so messy and we are so overwhelmed by the complexity and the untidy growth that only a few specialised denizens can cut their way through it,' he says. He cites the nuclear power station disaster at Three Mile Island in America where the operating staff did not have any way of understanding the messages and activities of the main control computer. Placing that order of responsibility on a few expert programmers is becoming a serious problem. It can only be overcome, Michie maintains, by a profound change in the programming of computers to simplify the software and give machines the power to reason, and above all, to explain what they are doing.

The accelerating speed of technological change, combined

with improved security procedures, Michie and others argue, may drive the final nail into the hacker's coffin – or they may force a change in his nature.

For the hacker, the haphazard evolution of complex software systems has provided both camouflage for and a challenge to his exploration. As Michie points out, only an elite group of professional programmers and dedicated hobbyists have been able to understand the myriad undergrowths of software. Organisations must pay dearly to tap that limited expertise. But, asks Michie, 'How would it be if we adopted languages that made sense to the ordinary practitioner?' So many man years and so much expertise have been invested in the evolution of the most commonly used languages, such as Cobol, that to throw them away and start again might seem far too expensive. Systems are maintained at enormous cost each year and so far it remains cheaper than starting from scratch again. But, Michie believes, like an overdarned piece of cloth, continual repairs will eventually become a false economy. New, highly structured programs will finally become the norm and they will create a clear computing landscape which will offer no hiding place for the hacker. Nevertheless, Michie accepts that such solutions would only come about in the long term.

Certainly, simpler operating systems might not form the same intellectual challenge for many hackers. However, the argument cuts both ways. Simpler operating systems could be exploited by a wider and less technically able public. And there will still be a significant number of specialists who will understand the innermost workings of a system, on a much more intimate basis than the average systems manager or security executive. If *they* choose to hack, they could be a much more serious threat than today's operating system hackers.

It is probably in the interest of the infant, though booming, security industry that hackers remain a perceived threat. Without them, suppliers of the add-on technical wizardry (such as smart cards and dongles), the consultants who advise on protecting systems, and those who rescue users from the scourge of viruses might find themselves out of a job. Those forecasting the imminent death of the hacker – pure and criminal – believe that increasingly sophisticated technology, especially in the field of telecommunications, will allow manufacturers to build in absolute protection against hackers, and that such gadgetry will make a hacker's life more difficult. Call-back systems which check the source of incoming calls may become prevalent. But the suppliers of enhanced security procedures do not fully take into account what it is that makes hackers tick. What is enjoyable for them is the challenge to their skills and ingenuity. The harder the manufacturers and users try to build up fortresses against them, the more determined they are likely to become in hacking them down. Hackers do not only know about software, which is certainly the weakest technological link in a system; many are knowledgeable about a wide variety of hardware. Above all, hackers are adept at exploiting the weaknesses introduced by the people using and looking after the systems.

If hacking does ever become too tortuous even for the most ardent enthusiast, there will always be new avenues to explore. Cellular phones are providing a new playground for the phreaker. A cellular phreaker can reportedly pick up another user's ID by reading it off the airwaves and then alter his own ID to the other user's account, thereby escaping bills. For the frustrated hacker there is already a new craze of fax hacking – or fax vandalism – where documents can be hijacked and altered over the telephone line. (In the US several states already have brought in laws against faxing unsolicited pages during peak business periods. Illegal junk-mail faxing could cost perpetrators $500 in Illinois. Following the massacre of students in Tienanmen Square in June 1989, there was a campaign in the West to saturate Chinese fax machines with sympathy messages. The campaign told magazine readers: 'You have the technology to affect history'. Information on the democracy movement sent in the 'Fax Attack' would be disseminated throughout China.) Echoing such trends is the observation attributed to William Gibson, author of the cult science fiction book *Neuromancer*, that: 'The street finds its own use for technology'.

Hackers may become so prevalent they will force more drastic solutions on telecommunication organisations. The only way to ensure that a computer, telephone or fax machine is not abused is to shut it away and not use it. For computer systems, at least, there may be a move back to the more secure but less economic stand-alone machines which have no links with the outside world. In March 1989 NASA was reported to be considering going off line and sending its confidential data on magnetic tapes because hackers had broken into its systems so frequently. 'In the US and Europe we have sites that are doing a range of different work, so almost anything would be vulnerable to hackers,' NASA's computer security policy manager said. Many sensitive government computer sites have never been on line for fear of the risk of penetration.

Hackers are not be the only ones intent on subverting telecommunications systems. Terrorists, it has frequently been suggested, may one day find logic bombs more effective than plastic explosives. Some intelligence organisations, such as GCHQ or the NSA, are rumoured to have been developing viruses for use in computer warfare against enemy states. Detective Superintendent Graham Seaby, who arrested Edward Singh, was not convinced that hacking could be eradicated easily. 'It's become like the arms race,' he said. 'Someone else is always developing something better.'

Systematic abuses of computer data bases in America were highlighted in *The Rise of the Computer State* by David Burnham, a *New York Times* journalist. (Burnham was the reporter who had arranged to meet Karen Silkwood while working on a story about a plutonium factory in Oklahoma. Silkwood died in a mysterious car crash on the way to meet him.) Burnham's book, written in 1980, was subtitled 'A Chilling Account of the Computer's Threat to Society'. He was most concerned by the uneven concentration of information created through computerisation. 'Is it reasonable to believe that a dedicated band of environmentalists, sending electronic smoke signals to each other via their home terminals, really will be able to effectively match the concentrated power of a giant oil company or committed government agency?' he asked. The relative growth in power of pcs, as compared to mainframes, and the organisation of environmental lobby groups may have weakened the comparison only slightly.

'The computer panders to the natural human instinct to desire more information about everything,' Burnham suggested. At the time of his book, computerised criminal records were being used more and more frequently by employers. People with only driving convictions could be unfairly stigmatised. Florida had even opened its criminal history records to anyone who would pay a search fee. The NSA had been responsible for a program which compiled 'watch-lists' of suspected subversives and intercepted international telegrams. The Agency, established in 1952, had also attempted to prevent academic computer scientists publishing papers on advances in encryption methods. Burnham's fears were part of a widespread fear of overpowerful state agencies. A US Government inquiry into privacy protection in the late 1970s opposed the state operation of electronic funds transfer systems as 'dangerous' and an 'unparalleled threat to privacy'. President Ford subsequently opposed a national EFT centre because it would give Federal government 'a highly effective tool for keeping track of people and enforcing "correct" behaviour'.

BEATING THE SYSTEM

Fears of computer intrusions into civil liberties in Britain have often focused on the Police National Computer. In 1989, Winchester Crown Court heard how private investigators using police contacts had regularly obtained access to the PNC. Three police officers and five private detectives were given suspended sentences at the end of the trial.

If hackers are indeed concerned about potential abuses of power or lax security, then some form of intermediary or honest broker may be necessary. Such understandings appear to have worked to an extent in West Germany, where some hacking is already illegal. Too many hackers, arrested by the police, are despised by their colleagues for giving information, although they are usually told there is no choice but to co-operate. As long as the relationship between hackers and authority is seen only as that of criminal to arresting officer, genuine concerns over inadequate computer security may remain stifled.

GLOSSARY

Applications software Programs for specialised computer functions, for example, word processors, spreadsheets and accounts.

Arpanet Advanced Research Projects Agency Network. Established as experimental network in America in the 1960s.

ATMs US acronym for Automatic Teller Machines. In the UK, hole-in-the-wall cash machines. Rely on PINs (Personal Identification Numbers) for controlling access.

Audit trail Log of events carried out in computer, used to trace past transactions or hacking incursions.

Backdoor Program usually inserted into computer's access control list allowing hackers to regain entry even if systems manager changes passwords. Works as long as systems manager does not spot the program.

BBSs Bulletin Boards Systems. Held on enthusiasts' home computers or set up surreptitiously in companies' mainframes. BBSs frequently contain electronic magazines assembled by groups of hackers, such as *TCSB* below:

Telecom Computer Security Bulletin   Volume One, Issue 1

An Introduction by Doctor Cypher and Necrovore

Welcome to the premier issue of *TCSB*. Since the demoralization of the underground there has been a rash of information hoarding and a

BEATING THE SYSTEM

blatant disregard of hacker ethics – this must stop if the underground is to survive. Our groups, Bellcore and Xtension, are almost misplaced in this day and age of the underground. We believe not in politics and images as do other groups, but rather in learning and sharing of knowledge. We don't call many boards any more. It churns our stomachs seeing what has become. *TCSB* is our way of emphasizing our beliefs and our solution to the problem. Hopefully the information provided in this and future issues of *TCSB* will prompt new happenings in the computer underworld. We can only hope.

TCSB is currently a fairly 'closed' publication. But we are not arrogant people. We will accept contributions as long as they are in character with the general style and format of *TCSB*. But you must contact either Doctor Cypher or Necrovore, and that can be potentially difficult. But good luck. *TCSB* is not on any sort of regular release schedule – such as other 'Hacker' mags are. We feel that if we begin to place deadlines on our releases then we will be stressed and will resort to releasing any file. That, in the end, affects the quality of the information and we want all information released in *TCSB* to be of the highest caliber possible. As such, the next issue of *TCSB* will be released when enough good files have been written.

While some of the information contained in these documents may be considered confidential Telco information, we at *TCSB* are not publishing this bulletin for the purpose of revealing trade secrets or any other implications of industrial espionage but rather a source of information that we hope you enjoy as much as we enjoy bringing it to you. In this issue you will find:

FILE	SIZE	AUTHOR	DESCRIPTION
TCSB.01	4156	Cypher/Necro	An Introduction to *TCSB* Volume One, Number 1
TCSB.02	3791	Doctor Cypher	There may be Gold in those Silver Boxes
TCSB.03	28696	Blade Runner	An Introduction to Itapac
TCSB.04	11539	Necrovore	PRIMOS CPL Directives Reference
TCSB.05	30447	Blade Runner	Introduction to Packet Switched Nets Part I
TCSB.06	27175	Blade Runner	Introduction to Packet Switched Nets Part II
TCSB.07	21327	The Usurper	Digital Transmission Techniques
TCSB.08	4348	Byte Man	Personal Telephone Security

TCSB.09	42598	Line Shadow	A Tutorial on the VAX/VMS Authorize Utility
TCSB.10	12128	Necrovore	PRIMOS RECV Parameters and DMSTK Formats
TCSB.11	8697	Mad Hacker	DEC Terminal Server Basics
TCSB.12	3308	Byteman	Z80 Memory Expansion for the hardware hacker

COMING NEXT ISSUE (whenever that may be):

Time to play God with your favorite system . . .

BCS British Computer Society.

Bildschirmtex German viewdata system, equivalent of Prestel in Britain or Minitel in France.

Blackbox or bluebox Used by phone phreaks. Tone generating machines which allowed users to make free telephone calls.

Byte A group of eight 'bits' of information – a data character. A 'bit' is the basic level of computer information – a binary value of 0 or 1.

Cap'n Crunch Alias of John Draper, a once notorious US phreaker. Now a West Coast computer consultant.

CCTA Central Computing and Telecommunications Agency. The UK Government's computer resource centre which oversaw creation of the Government Data Network.

Chaos Computer Club Hamburg-based West German hacker and computer enthusiasts association.

CHAPS Clearing House Automatic Payments System. The main electronic funds transfer network for inter-bank transactions in the UK.

Chip Basic hardware building blocks of modern computers; minute pieces of silicon containing memory or microprocessors.

Cocom Co-ordinating Committee for Multilateral Export Controls, based in Paris. A US-dominated grouping of NATO nations (as well as Japan) established to restrict flow of high technology to Eastern bloc countries.

Data Protection Act Requires all information held on computer to be registered with the Data Protection Registrar. There are exceptions for categories of government data. Allows members of the public the right to see the entries concerning them held on data bases.

Default passwords Standard passwords installed in computers when sold to customers. Default passwords should be changed by systems managers but often are not.

DES Data Encryption Standard. Encryption method approved by US standards authorities, overseen by the National Security Agency.

Dongle Hardware security device designed to control acces to computers.

Eavesdropping The process of illicitly picking up electromagnetic radiation emissions from computers and reconstituting them to discover what is on the screen.

EFT/POS Electronic Funds Transfer at Point of Sale. System for allowing cash to be directly debited by shops from customers' bank accounts as items are bought. Still at experimental stage.

Encryption algorithm Mathematical key or formula used to encode and decode files messages.

FAST Federation Against Software Theft. Organisation formed by computer and software manufacturers to stop unauthorised use of copyrighted programs.

GCHQ Government Communications Headquarters at Cheltenham. Equivalent of US National Security Agency. Electronics intelligence monitoring centre.

GDN Government Data Network. Links up Whitehall and central government ministries around Britain.

Hacking handles Hackers' pseudonyms. Tend to show influence of science fiction and computer terminology – one continental group calls itself the Swiss Cracking Association. Other individual examples include:

Megabyte	ByteMan	Blade Runner
Blackhack	Chippy	Line Shadow
Electron	Mad Hacker	The Usurper
Slugbreath	Doc Telecom	Backlash
Tekno	Felix The Hack	Par
Robot	Logex	Wiz
Belbel	Force	SkyHook

BEATING THE SYSTEM

Homebrew Computing Club US West Coast/Silicon Valley computer club embodying the notion of hackers in its first computer sense as creators of personal computers.

Internet US-based computer network.

Janet Joint Academic Network. Connects up universities, polytechnics and colleges throughout the United Kingdom. Has gateways onto the major public data networks and academic networks abroad.

LANs Local Area Networks.

Logic bomb Program inserted into host computer which is set to go off on a specific date or after a system has been accessed a certain number of times. Can be programmed to erase files or perform less malicious tasks.

Mainframes Larger commercial computer systems. The next size down is the minicomputers, then the personal computer (pc). With advances in technology, smaller machines are becoming increasingly powerful.

Modem Modulater/demodulator. Device for converting signals for transmission and reception across the telephone line. Allows home computers to be connected to networks around the world.

NASA National Aeronautical and Space Agency. US space centre whose data bases and networks have been penetrated by hackers. NASA is connected to the international academic network SPAN (Space Physics Analysis Network).

NCSC US National Computer Security Centre.

NSA US National Security Agency. Electronics intelligence and communications monitoring service. The American equivalent of GCHQ.

NUA/NUI Network User Address on a packet switch network. Network User Identity, equivalent to password and allowing permission to use network.

Operating Systems Software in computer; the machine's main internal communications language. In computer architecture, operating systems are above the hardware and below the applications programs.

OSI Open Systems Interconnect. Movement to produce common communications standards enabling different computers to link up to one another.

PAD Packet Assembler/disassembler. Creates and unpacks data packets for transmission and receipt across packet-switching networks. Permits home-computer users to connect up to packet-switching networks.

Password A request for a password will appear on the remote user's screen immediately after logging on to most systems.

Phreaking Illicitly obtaining free phone calls from public telephone systems.

Prestel Viewdata or videotex system. Provides variety of services through its pages.

PSS Packet Switch Stream. Main UK packet-switching network. In the US similar networks are Telenet and Tymnet.

Secret Service US Intelligence agency associated with Treasury Department. Formally specialised in providing presidential bodyguards and dealing with counterfeit and fraud cases. By extension has been empowered to deal with hacking investigations.

Smartcards Similar to bank credit cards, with information identifying an individual recorded on a microprocessor. Used to control access to computers.

Staatschutz West German equivalent of Britain's Special Branch. The Verfassungschutz is responsible for counterintelligence; similar to MI5.

SWIFT Society for Worldwide Interbank Financial Transactions. The international network connecting banks around the world. A larger scale CHAPS.

Tiger team Groups of tame hackers, paid to attempt to break into a specified system to test security measures. More common in the US but have been used in Britain.

Trojan horse Program hidden inside apparently normal file or software which is introduced to host system. Can be triggered to cause damage or alter information.

Virus Program which cna reproduce itself within computers by attaching itself to other programs. Can be passed from one machine to another by hiding in software files. Usually created with malicious intent to damage computer hard disks and erase information.

Worm Program similar to a virus, but designed only to reproduce itself (segment by segment like a worm) within computers and across networks. Unlike viruses, a worm is not programmed to erase or alter files, but can create chaos by soaking up machine space and crashing systems.